SHAKESPEARE AND COMPANY

by
Sylvia
Beach

New Edition

Introduction by James Laughlin

University of Nebraska Press   Lincoln

First Bison Book, New Edition printing: 1991
Most recent printing indicated by the last digit below:
10   9   8   7   6   5   4

Library of Congress Cataloging-in-Publication Data
Beach, Sylvia.
Shakespeare and Company / by Sylvia Beach.—New ed. / introduction by
James Laughlin.
p.   cm.
"A Bison book."
Reprint. Originally published: New York: Harcourt, Brace, c1959.
Includes index.
ISBN 0-8032-6097-0 (pbk.)
1. Shakespeare and Company—History.   2. Booksellers and bookselling—
France—Paris—History—20th century.   3. Authors and publishers—
France—Paris—History—20th century.   4. Literature publishing—
France—Paris—History—20th century.   5. Americans—France—Paris—
History—20th century.   6. Beach, Sylvia—Homes and haunts—France—
Paris.   7. Paris (France)—Intellectual life—20th century.   I. Title.
Z305.S45B42   1991
381'.45002'0944—dc20
91-15230   CIP

To the memory of
Adrienne Monnier

CONTENTS

ILLUSTRATIONS

Introduction to the New Edition
By James Laughlin

"Publisher of the most important novel of this century . . . probably the best known woman in Paris . . . certainly one of the important figures in contemporary letters . . . America's single most important literary outpost in Europe . . . for twenty years the best known bookshop in the world." These are the terms in which the historian of publishing Hugh Ford describes Sylvia Beach and her Shakespeare and Company bookshop.

When I think back to my first extended sojourn in Paris—that would have been in 1934–35—I remember many pleasant and often exciting people but none come back to me more vividly than those two remarkable literary ladies Gertrude Stein and Sylvia Beach. Both were American. Gertrude Stein was born in 1874 in Allegheny, Pennsylvania, just across the river from Pittsburgh, where my own paternal grandparents lived on Lincoln Avenue. Sylvia Beach was younger, born in 1887, in a Presbyterian parsonage in Princeton, New Jersey, where all good Laughlin boys were sent to college (except for the black sheep who strayed to Harvard), as commemorated by a pseudo-Gothic Laughlin Hall, the gift to the university of the same grandfather.

How Miss Stein and Miss Beach came to live in Paris, one in

the rue de Fleurus and one in the rue de L'Odéon, each not far from the Luxembourg gardens on the Left Bank, are rather long stories that need not concern us here. (My favorite biography of Stein is James R. Mellow: *Charmed Circle: Gertrude Stein and Company*, New York, Praeger, 1974; the standard work on Beach is Noel Riley Fitch: *Sylvia Beach and the Lost Generation*, New York, Norton, 1983.) Suffice it to say that by the fall of 1934, when I took up residence in a windowless cubicle in an insurance office near the Champ de Mars (where the rent was eight francs a week) Miss Stein and Miss Beach, each in her different way, had by sheer energy of personality, made Paris, at least such parts of it as were frequented by expatriate Americans, their unchallenged domain. But, as Miss Stein would have said, they didn't do it together. And each had strong support, Miss Stein from Alice B. Toklas, and Sylvia Beach from Adrienne Monnier, the motherly (or so I thought: she once sewed on an important button for me) lady who ran the French bookshop across the street from Shakespeare and Company.

Gertrude Stein was one of the first customers at Shakespeare and Company. She complained that she couldn't find two of her favorite books, *The Girl of the Limberlost* and *The Trail of the Lonesome Pine*, but was placated when she found her own *Tender Buttons* in the shopwindow. There were expeditions with Sylvia's companion, Adrienne Monnier, to the country in Gertrude's little Ford "Godiva" and many dinners in the rue de Fleurus with American writers who were afraid to approach the awesome Miss Stein on their own. All went well until Sylvia published *Ulysses*. Then a freeze descended and "the flowers of friendship faded friendship faded," to quote the famous Stein poem.

I can vouch for this anecdote. I had a similar experience with the literary monolith. The summer that I was working for Stein at Bilignin, her place in the country, all was going well till she caught me reading Proust. She was deeply offended. "J," she asked, "how can you read such stuff? Don't you know that Proust and Joyce copied their books from my *Making of Ameri-*

cans?" But the rift did not last and the final word from the oracle was the poem that she wrote about Shakespeare and Company, "Rich and Poor in English." It's a long poem but here are two excerpts from it. (The entire poem can be found on pages 95–97 of Gertrude's book, *Painted Lace*.)

RICH AND POOR IN ENGLISH. TO SUBSCRIBE IN
  FRENCH AND OTHER LATIN LANGUAGES
          (SYLVIA BEACH)

Not a country not a door send them away to sit on the floor.
Cakes. This is not the world. Can you remember.
  Can any one remember much.
  Say it to touch an edition say it to bury a collection.
  When this you see remember me.
  How often can we sing it.
  I have almost a little burr.
  I have almost a country there.
  And yet the strangest part of it is that Russia continues
      her tradition.
****

Can I dare to say that the Atlantic will like Poles who float and
    after that a boat. A boat to say I may. Yes.
Richard Poor.
A sister.
Is a sister necessarily older.
The rich and poor squeak like a canary bird.
I am going to tell a story about the bird.

Sylvia's first intention was that Shakespeare and Company would be primarily a lending library of English-language books. The "company" would be her subscribers, the "bunnies" as she called them after the French "abbonés." Gradually, and especially when the tourists began to seek it out, it became a shop for selling books as well as lending them, and finally when Sylvia published Joyce's *Ulysses* a publishing house as well. It also became a *poste restante* for Hemingway and other writers who had no fixed address in Paris. The first location of Shakespeare and Company when it opened in 1919 was at 8 rue Dupuytren, premises that had once been a laundry. But by the time I knew it the shop had been moved to more spacious quarters at 12 rue de l'Odéon.

Unlike most booksellers today, Sylvia encouraged browsing. Shakespeare and Company was not just a business, it was a cause, the cause of the best literature. She had been a voracious reader in her youth and she had taste that she wanted to share. To encourage browsing she had made a trip to the flea market and brought back a number of heavy old armchairs which, as well I recall, were very comfortable. Bookshelves were only on the walls. The central part of the shop was open like a living room and good light came in from the windows. When you entered the shop the eye focused immediately on a display of photographs on two of the walls over the bookshelves. Whitman, Poe, and Wilde (and two fine Blake drawings) had the places of honor but every first-class contemporary writer was represented—Joyce, Pound, Lawrence, William Carlos Williams, and many more. There was a rack for all the best literary magazines of the day: *The Little Review, Broom, The Dial, This Quarter, Poetry, The Egoist, The New English Review,* and of course, *transition,* in which Eugene Jolas and his group were carrying on "the revolution of the word," to which I dedicated the first New Directions annual in 1936. To make up for no central heating in winter there was a stove in the shop. There was also a little bedroom off the main room where Sylvia or a bedless writer could spend the night.

Sylvia was a birdlike little figure but she had the strength and energy of a thoroughbred racehorse. She was a chain-smoker and constantly in motion. I remember that quickness of movement as she darted about the shop, the brightness of eye, her sense of humor (she loved puns) and her gift for repartee. Never a dull moment at Shakespeare and Company.

Here is Hemingway's description of Sylvia (from *A Moveable Feast*):

Sylvia had a lively, sharply sculptured face, brown eyes that were as alive as a small animal's and as gay as a young girl's, and wavy brown hair that was brushed back from her fine forehead and cut thick below her ears and at the line of the collar of the brown velvet jacket she wore. She had pretty legs and she was kind, cheerful and interested, and loved to make jokes and gossip. No one that I ever knew was nicer to me.

And here is Hugh Ford's description of Sylvia:

For those who came to Shakespeare and Company expecting to find a renegade with advanced prurient tastes there was bound to be a sudden reversal of expectation. Even her attire suggested restraint and a no-nonsense approach to things. Removed from her bibliophilistic surroundings she might have passed for a corporation secretary, or a schoolmistress, prim, forceful, formidable. She preferred mannish clothing; a tailor-made velvet jacket, a bow tie set in a low white collar, a felt hat, a shirt of nondescript dark cloth, and sensible American shoes. . . . Her hair she kept neatly crimped. A sufferer all her life from poor eyesight . . . she wore steel-rimmed glasses that gave her features a touch of severity.

I'm not in a position to say much about the Beach-Joyce relationship. On my one visit with Joyce I was trying to smoke out whether he had really gotten the monologue intérieur from the venerable Edouard Dujardin's *Les Lauriers sont coupés* (which New Directions published in 1938). His answers on that were delphic to say the least. What the great artificer wanted to talk about was the names of all the country towns near Pittsburgh and the names of all the streams, no matter how small, that watered them. But nothing short of an almost religious devotion could have made Sylvia so patient as she was with Joyce's scrambled manuscript and proof corrections.

The indifferent parody of the lines from *Two Gentlemen of Verona* with which Joyce offered his thanks to Sylvia on the publication day of *Ulysses* is a matter of record.

> Who is Sylvia, what is she
> That all our scribes commend her?
> Yankee, young and brave is she
> The West this grace did lend her
> That all books might published be. . .

and so forth for two more lame stanzas. He might really for the year's grief given have tried a bit harder than that. But "James Jheezus," as Pound used to call him, was seldom very recognizant of benefactions except to his great patron, Harriet Weaver. Skim through the volume of the Pound-Joyce correspondence. There you will find dozens of letters from Pound in which Ez is pulling every possible string to get help for the then impoverished Joyce, trying to find publishers and patrons for him, even collecting clothes and prescribing for Joyce's eye trouble, but not a single line from Joyce expressing any interest in Pound's work. I dare say I'm too hard on the great man. From Sylvia's account of her hero, you will learn that he had perfect manners and was nice to everyone.

In later years I didn't have much time to spend in Paris, being busy with New Directions and my work for the Ford Foundation, but I kept in touch with Sylvia by mail and we were involved in two very pleasant publishing projects. In 1929 Sylvia and Joyce had conceived the idea of an exegetic symposium on *Finnegans Wake* (then known as the *Work in Progress.*) She brought it out in 1929. It bore the very Joycean title of *Our Exagmination round His Factification for Incamination of Work in Progress* and included pieces by Samuel Beckett, Stuart Gilbert, Eugene Jolas, William Carlos Williams, and a number of others. Among these was a "mystery" piece signed by a "Vladimir Dixon," which began:

"Dear Mister Germ's Choice: in gutter dispear I am taking my pen toilet you know that I am so disturd by my inhumility to onthorstand most of the implocations constrained in your work . . . that I am writing you mysterre Shame's Voice, to let you no how bed I feeloxerab out it all."

Some years later Sylvia wrote to tell me that she had overprinted her edition of *Exagmination* and would I take over some of her copies for distribution by New Directions, which, for the sport of it, I was delighted to do.

Our other collaboration, this in 1949, was our own edition of Sylvia's fine translation of *A Barbarian in Asia* by her good friend the poet Henri Michaux. As a young man Michaux had made an extended trip through the Far East, setting down his observations and illuminations on the Asian cultures with a wonderful irony and wit that foreshadowed what he would later do with our own culture in his poetry.

I have a special personal debt to Sylvia. Reading *Shakespeare and Company* gave me the clue for the form I needed to use in my own little book of recollections. I would do just as she had done. Put the name of a person or a topic at the head of the page and then type in what was remembered about him or it. No need to worry about structure or chronology. Pound, who was much besought by publishers to write his autobiography, always said that if a man wrote his meeemoirs that was a sign he was finished. Well, I guess I'm finished. The temptations of memory are too great to be withstood. And I'm trying to do it the way Sylvia did it.

How did it all end? When the war came Sylvia was urged to return to the States but she didn't want to leave Adrienne and her other friends or close down Shakespeare and Company. George Wickes tells the story in his book *Americans in Paris:*

Sylvia Beach remained in Paris through the German occupation and lived there until her death in 1962. She kept the bookstore open until one day in 1941, when a German officer wanted to buy the copy of *Finnegans Wake* on display in the window and when she refused to sell, threatened to confiscate all her possessions. In a matter of hours Sylvia and her friends moved all the contents of the shop into an upstairs apartment and its name was painted over. Shakespeare and Company no longer existed.

Shakespeare and Company never reopened. Sylvia had to spend six months in an internment camp. After her release everyone urged her to reopen the shop but she didn't have the heart for it. Happily, she did decide to write this book, the best memorial that her life's work could possibly have.

Shakespeare and Company

ONE

"for Who-is-silvier—"

My father, the Reverend Sylvester Woodbridge Beach, D.D., was a Presbyterian minister who for seventeen years was pastor of the First Presbyterian Church in Princeton, New Jersey.

According to an article in *Munsey's Magazine* on curious family trees in America, the Woodbridges, Father's maternal ancestors, were clergymen from father to son for some twelve or thirteen generations. My sister Holly, who prefers the truth at all costs, has gone into and, alas, debunked the story. She has reduced the ministers to nine, and we have to be content with that.

My mother, an Orbison, like some character in mythology, sprang from a spring. That is, a certain ancestor of hers, Captain James Harris, poking around in his backyard, discovered an excellent spring, and on the spot laid out the town in the Alleghenies called Bellefonte. It was Mrs. Harris who thought of the name. I prefer the story Mother used to tell me of Lafayette dropping in to get a drink of water from the spring and exclaiming, *"Belle fontaine!"* Though it's not likely that a Frenchman would be asking for a glass of water.

Mother was born, not in her mountainy town in Pennsylvania, but in Rawalpindi, India, where her father was a medical missionary. Grandfather Orbison brought his family home to

3

Bellefonte. His widow brought up their four children there and spent the rest of her life in the town, where she was almost as much venerated as the famous spring.

Mother attended Bellefonte Academy. Her Latin teacher was a tall, handsome young man, recently graduated from Princeton College and Princeton Theological Seminary, Sylvester Woodbridge Beach. She was only sixteen. They became engaged, but waited two years to get married.

Father's first call was to Baltimore, where I was born. The next call was to Bridgeton, New Jersey, where Father was pastor of the First Presbyterian Church for twelve years.

I was about fourteen when Father took the whole family to Paris—Mother, my two younger sisters, Holly and Cyprian, and myself. Father had been asked to take charge of what were called the Students' Atelier Reunions. This was before the days of the fine club for American students in the Boulevard Raspail. Every Sunday evening, in a big studio in Montparnasse, American students came under home influence. That is, Father gave a sensible talk, and some of the most brilliant singers of the time, such as Mary Garden and Charles Clark, the great cellist Pablo Casals, and other artists gave their services to this work. Even Löie Fuller. She came not to dance but to talk about her dancing. I remember her as a stumpy, rather plain girl from Chicago, wearing glasses, the schoolmarm type, telling about the experiments she was making with radium in connection with her lighting system. She was dancing at the Moulin Rouge at the time, as I remember, and making a sensation. When you saw her there, the stoutish woman you knew as Löie Fuller was transformed. With two outstretched sticks, she manipulated five hundred meters of swirling stuff, flames enveloped her, and she was consumed. Finally, all that remained were a few ashes.

Father and Mother loved France and the French, though we knew very few French people because Father's work threw us mostly with our compatriots. Father got on famously with the French; I think he was a Latin at heart. He made a great effort to learn the language. A Deputy friend of his gave him lessons, and he was soon able to read and write perfectly, but the pronunciation—ah! that was another matter. We used to hear from the next room the Deputy's efforts to teach him the French "u." First we heard the Deputy's "u" followed by Father's "OOH," louder but no nearer. And so it went on.

Paris was paradise to Mother; an Impressionist painting. She enjoyed getting up the programs for the student reunions; that was her job. And she liked the company of the artists.

The important event for me in those first years in Paris was meeting my friend, a lifelong friend, Carlotta Welles. You imagine, of course, that, with that name, Carlotta was Italian, but the name was only an accident. After her birth, which took place in Alassio, her father tried to declare her as "Charlotte," but at the courthouse it was translated into "Carlotta" when it was registered in the book. Mr. Welles used to introduce Carlotta as "our little Italian." Since she was a stout American patriot, that made her very mad. Mr. Welles represented Western Electric in Paris, and he had opened branches of the firm all over Europe and the Far East. He was a pioneer in electricity, and a big name in that field.

The Welleses were our compatriots but they lived in France, and it was through Carlotta and her family that I learned to know it. They had a country place down in Touraine on the river Cher near the town of Bourré. They shared it with their friends, and the Beaches were among these lucky friends. Mr. Welles's pastimes were building up a wonderful library, into which he disappeared for hours at a time; and building up a fine cellar—he was a connoisseur of wines. He had to wait till Carlotta grew up and married Jim Briggs to have someone in the family he could discuss vintages with. Jim Briggs knew at least as much about wines as his father-in-law, and certainly a great deal more about the French cuisine.

The chateau above the winding little Cher was set in a landscape that was like an old French tapestry: the two houses, the new and the old; the gardens that went down from terrace to terrace; the little wood going up the hill; the walled kitchen garden down near the bank of the river; and the island you crossed over to in a punt. All of this fascinated the little Beaches.

I stayed for some time with Carlotta when the Welleses' doctor advised them to take her out of school and keep her outdoors. I was invited to keep Carlotta company, and that was the way our long, long friendship began. Carlotta was the first bird watcher I ever knew, and this independent, rather sarcastic little girl in a gingham dress—all of the Welleses were sarcastic—spent much of her time perched in some big tree spying on the birds through field glasses.

During this first interval in Europe I got the few months of schooling I ever had. Holly and I went to a school in Lausanne, where, owing to the curious notions of the two ladies who directed it, the discipline was better suited to a bunch of incorrigibles in a reformatory than to a lot of meek maidens. I learned a little French grammar, but I was miserable, and soon Mother brought me home. It was then that I went down to stay with Carlotta in Bourré, and I would have been completely happy if it had not been for the thought of Holly, still at the school, still walking out twice a day in twos, never allowed to look out of the window at the Lake of Geneva, or to address a word to anyone except on the walks; and singing with a cork between her teeth to keep her mouth open. But Holly was a Stoic.

From Paris we went to Princeton. Father was delighted to be called to Princeton, for he had spent his student years there, and looked on it as home. Mother, too, was happy. Princeton was the town she would have chosen to live in if she had been asked. We settled down in the Colonial parsonage on Library Place. Did the name influence my choice of a career in the book business? Princeton, with its trees and birds, is more a leafy, flowery park than a town, and the Beach family considered itself lucky.

My friend Annis Stockton was an authority on Princeton history, and with Annis I visited the battlefields in the Stocktons' cart drawn by Reedy, with the dachshund Rock squeezed up on the seat between us. It was Annis who told me that the horses of Washington's staff had munched their oats in the pews of the First Presbyterian Church. Annis was the descendant of Signers of the Declaration, and portraits of her ancestors Benjamin Franklin and Sarah Bache looked down from the Stocktons' walls.

Even in Father's congregations we had history-makers, past and future: the Grover Clevelands, the James Garfields, and the Woodrow Wilsons. Grover Cleveland was a charming, peace-loving man. He had retired to Princeton to live quietly with his family around him. Mother had met Mrs. Cleveland, who was a beautiful woman, when they were brides. The children, two boys and two girls, had lovely manners, the kind you never see any more.

As for Woodrow Wilson, he was a scholarly man who would also have liked a peaceful life, but things turned out otherwise. He was not a talker, but what he did say was so interesting that everybody listened to him. His daughters adored him. He was a home-lover, and if he went away, Margaret, Jessie, and Eleanor moped around the house till he came back. Margaret sang, and, because the Wilsons had no piano, she came to the parsonage to have my sister Cyprian accompany her.

By an amusing coincidence, which Woodrow Wilson remarked upon to my sister Holly, the special railroad car in which he left Princeton for Washington was named "Holly Beach."

Even after the Wilsons moved to Washington, they always considered Father their pastor. They sent for him to perform the ceremony in the White House when both Jessie and Eleanor were married; and, at Wilson's request, Father was one of those who officiated at the President's funeral.

During the years in Princeton, we often went to France for visits or longer stays—sometimes the whole family, sometimes just one or two of us. We had a veritable passion for France. A friend in Princeton who shared this passion was Margaret Sloane, the daughter of Professor William Sloane, who had written a life of Napoleon. Margaret was delighted when, on a hot Sunday morning at the First Presbyterian Church, she saw my sister Cyprian seat herself in our front pew and open a large fan decorated with a black cat and the name of a famous cabaret in Paris, *Au Chat Noir*.

Mr. Ben W. Huebsch remembers a certain Sylvia Beach who came up to New York from Princeton around 1916 to consult him on the subject of a career. I admired him very much, but that was no excuse for taking his time. He was extremely kind, and encouraged me in what, as I recall, was a vague plan for a bookshop. I don't doubt that already there was a mysterious bond between Mr. Huebsch and a future follower of his in the Joycean field.

TWO

Palais Royal

I went to Spain in 1916, and spent some months there. In 1917, I went on to Paris. For some time, I had had a particular interest in contemporary French writing. Now I wanted to pursue my studies at the source.

My sister Cyprian was also in France. Cyprian had wanted to become an opera singer, but, with a war in progress, the time was not propitious. She had turned to the films instead. Soon after I arrived, we joined forces and lived for a while in the Palais Royal. Cyprian had many friends in the theatrical world, and it was through them that she discovered this interesting place, which was frequented by actors and, for some reason, the Spanish. We had rooms in the hotel at the far end of the Palais Royal. It was there, we were told, that John Howard Payne had written "Home, Sweet Home." To think that his wistful " 'Mid pleasures and palaces" had been written in such a shabby old "palace"! Right next door was the Palais Royal Theatre, where the naughtiest plays in Paris were put on.

In spite of the theatre and one or two bookshops dealing mostly in erotica, the Palais Royal was at this time fairly respectable. It had been otherwise in the old days, when, according to a guidebook I picked up, the Duc d'Orléans, or, rather, his son, the Regent, lived there and gave those famous parties.

9

My guidebook also said that he hung paintings by the Masters on his walls and that he took in Czar Peter the Great when he came to Paris. The Palais Royal did not reform with the passing years. Its arcades were frequented by the rakes, and no wonder, what with its "jewelry shops, lending libraries, and the courtesans who paraded their half-naked charms." Finally, the Palais Royal attracted such an undesirable crowd that it had to be "moralized," whereupon it lost, of course, "much of its interest and popularity." But we found it interesting.

Our windows looked over the gardens. There was a fountain in the middle, and, beyond, stood Rodin's statue of Victor Hugo. The neighborhood babies excavated the walks with their little spades amid clouds of dust; the old trees were full of songbirds; the cats, who were the real owners of the gardens, kept an eye on the birds.

A balcony ran all the way around the Palais, and our windows opened on to it. If you were curious to see how your neighbor lived, all you had to do was walk over and into his window—which was what happened to us. One evening, as we sat near the open window, a blithe young man appeared on the balcony and stepped into the room with his hand cordially extended. Smiling delightedly, he introduced himself as one of the artistes at the theatre next door. Very inhospitably, I fear, we pushed our visitor out and closed the window; then, by the time he had disappeared in the direction of the bell that could be heard ringing to announce the next act, we were dressed and down at the box office of the Théâtre du Palais Royal. The manager listened politely to our complaint, though he had difficulty keeping a straight face. He asked us to describe the offender, but our description of "a dark young man with a mustache" might fit any of his artistes, he said, so he suggested that we seat ourselves in a proscenium box and point out the guilty one as soon as he came on the stage. This we did, exclaiming "*Le voilà!*" Thereupon the whole audience, and the actors, including our visitor, began to laugh; but at us, not at the play. And we joined them, I must confess.

Cyprian was so beautiful that you couldn't blame a fellow for coming in the window without an invitation. And the poor girl couldn't stroll around in Paris, as she liked to do, without being pestered by some follower or other. She was immediately recognized by little boys as "Belles Mirettes," a character in a serial film called "Judex," shown in weekly episodes at movie theatres all over Paris, and a crowd of her fans sprang up wherever she went. Our worst experience of this sort occurred when we went to hear some lovely old French music at Notre Dame. The choirboys caught sight of "Belles Mirettes" and pointed at her, whispering, until, taking pity on the choirmaster, a young Father we admired very much, we got up and went out.

Among my sister's admirers was the poet Aragon, then active in the Dada movement. After raving about his passion for the *momie* of Cleopatra at a Parisian museum, Aragon told me he had now transferred his admiration to Cyprian. Later, in search of Cyprian, he made frequent visits to my bookshop and sometimes recited for me his Alphabet poem and the one called *"La Table."* "The Alphabet" was simply that, recited slowly from beginning to end. As for *"La Table,"* it consisted of the words *"la table"* repeated to the end of the poem.

During the nightly air raids, Cyprian and I had the choice of catching the flu in the cellar or enjoying the view from the balcony. We usually chose the latter. More frightening was "Big Bertha," the Germans' pet gun, which raked the streets during the day. One afternoon—it was Good Friday—I was at the Palais de Justice attending the trial of a militant pacifist schoolteacher friend of mine. Suddenly, there was a crash, the trial was suspended, and, rushing out, we saw that the church of Saint Gervais, just across the river, had been hit. A lot of people who had come from all over town to hear the famous choir were killed and a very interesting old church sadly damaged.

The Little Gray Bookshop of A. Monnier

One day at the Bibliothèque Nationale, I noticed that one of the reviews—Paul Fort's *Vers et Prose*, I think it was—could be purchased at A. Monnier's bookshop, 7 rue de l'Odéon, Paris VI. I had not heard the name before, nor was the Odéon quarter familiar to me, but suddenly something drew me irresistibly to the spot where such important things in my life were to happen. I crossed the Seine and was soon in the rue de l'Odéon, with its theatre at the end reminding me somehow of Colonial houses in Princeton. Halfway up the street on the left side was a little gray bookshop with "A. Monnier" above the door. I gazed at the exciting books in the window, then, peering into the shop, saw all around the walls shelves containing volumes in the glistening "crystal paper" overcoats that French books wear while waiting, often for a long time, to be taken to the binder's. There were also some interesting portraits of writers here and there.

At a table sat a young woman. A. Monnier herself, no doubt. As I hesitated at the door, she got up quickly and opened it, and, drawing me into the shop, greeted me with much warmth. This was surprising in France, where people are as a rule reserved with strangers, but I learned that it was characteristic of Adrienne Monnier, particularly if the strangers were Americans. I was disguised in a Spanish cloak and hat, but Adrienne knew at once that I was American. "I like America very much," she said. I replied that I liked France very much. And, as our future collaboration proved, we meant it.

As I stood near the open door, a high wind suddenly blew my Spanish hat off my head and into the middle of the street, and away it went bowling. A. Monnier rushed after it, going very fast for a person in such a long skirt. She pounced on it just as it was about to be run over, and, after brushing it off carefully, handed it to me. Then we both burst out laughing.

Adrienne Monnier was stoutish, her coloring fair, almost like a Scandinavian's, her cheeks pink, her hair straight and brushed back from her fine forehead. Most striking were her eyes. They were blue-gray and slightly bulging, and reminded me of William Blake's. She looked extremely alive. Her dress, of a style that suited her perfectly, somebody once described as a cross between a nun's and a peasant's: a long, full skirt down to her feet, and a sort of tight-fitting velvet waistcoat over a white silk blouse. She was in gray and white like her bookshop. Her voice was rather high; she was descended from mountaineers who must have hailed each other from peak to peak.

Adrienne Monnier and I sat down, and, of course, talked about books. She told me that she had always been interested in American writing. She had procured everything that was available in translation for her library, beginning with her favorite, Benjamin Franklin. I told her she would like *Moby Dick*, but it had not yet been translated into French. (Jean Giono's translation appeared later, and Adrienne did like *Moby Dick*.) She had not read the contemporary American writers. They were not known at the time in France.

In modern French writing I was only a beginner, but a good beginner, Adrienne thought, when she heard that I was a lover of Valéry's work and possessed a copy of *La Jeune Parque*. We agreed that I must go on with Jules Romains, whom I had begun reading in America, and she offered to help me with Claudel. So I was enrolled as a member of A. Monnier's library, La Maison des Amis des Livres, for one year—and for many.

During the last months of the war, as the guns boomed closer and closer to Paris, I spent many hours in the little gray bookshop of Adrienne Monnier. French authors were always dropping in—some of them from the front and in uniform— and getting into lively discussions with her; one of them was always sitting beside her table.

Then there were the readings, which I never missed. Members of the library were invited to La Maison des Amis des

Livres to hear unpublished manuscripts read by the authors or, as when Gide read Valéry, by their friends. Crowded into the little shop and almost on top of the reader at his table, we listened breathlessly.

We heard Jules Romains, in uniform, read his peace poem, "Europe." Valéry talked about Poe's *Eureka*. André Gide read more than once. Others who read for us were Jean Schlumberger, Valery Larbaud, and Léon-Paul Fargue. Occasionally, there was a musical program with Erik Satie and Francis Poulenc; then—but that was after Shakespeare and Company came to join the Maison des Amis des Livres—James Joyce.

I believe that I was the only American to discover the rue de l'Odéon and participate in its exciting literary life at that time. I owe a great deal of the success of my bookshop to the help of all those French friends I made at Adrienne Monnier's.

At intervals, I varied my life in the literary world. One whole summer I worked as a volunteer farm hand (*volontaire agricole*); all male farmers were at the front. After harvesting the wheat, I picked grapes in the vineyards of Touraine. Then my sister Holly managed to get me a job in the American Red Cross. We went to Belgrade, where for nine months I distributed pajamas and bath towels among the valiant Serbs. In July 1919, I was back in Paris.

THREE

A Bookshop of My Own

I had long wanted a bookshop, and by now it had become an obsession. I dreamed of a French bookshop but it was to be a branch of Adrienne's and in New York. I wanted to help the French writers I admired so much to become more widely known in my country. I soon realized, however, that my mother's little savings, which she was willing to risk on my venture, would be insufficient to cover the cost of a shop in New York. Very regretfully, I had to abandon this fascinating idea.

I thought Adrienne Monnier would be disappointed to hear of the downfall of our scheme of a French place, a branch of hers, in my country. On the contrary, she was delighted. And so, in a minute, was I, as right before our eyes my bookshop turned into an American one in Paris. My capital would go much further there. Rents were lower and so was the cost of living in those days.

I saw all these advantages. Moreover, I was extremely fond of Paris, I must confess, and this was no small inducement to settle down there and become a Parisian. Then, too, Adrienne had had four years of experience as a bookseller. She had opened her shop in the midst of a war and, moreover, kept it going. She promised to advise me in my first steps; also to send me lots of customers. The French, as I knew, were very eager to get hold of our new writers, and it seemed to me that a little American bookshop on the Left Bank would be welcome.

The difficulty was to find a vacant shop in Paris. I might have had to wait some time before finding what I wanted if Adrienne hadn't noticed that there was a place for rent in the rue Dupuytren, a little street just around the corner from the rue de l'Odéon. Busy though she was with her library, her publications, and her own writing, she somehow found time to help me with my preparations. We hurried to the rue Dupuytren, where, at No. 8—there were only about ten numbers in this hilly little street—was a shop with the shutters up and a sign saying "*Boutique a louer.*" It had once been a laundry, said Adrienne, pointing to the words "*gros*" and "*fin*" on either side of the door, meaning they did up both sheets and fine linen. Adrienne, who was rather plump, placed herself under the "*gros*" and told me to stand under the "*fin*." "That's you and me," she said.

We hunted up the concierge, an old lady in a black lace cap, who lived in a sort of cage between two floors, as concierges do in these old Paris houses, and she showed us the premises. *My* premises, as, without hesitation, I decided they would be. There were two rooms, with a glass door between them, and steps leading into the one at the back. There was a fireplace in the front room; the laundress's stove, with the irons on it, had stood in front of it. The poet Léon-Paul Fargue drew a picture of the stove as it must have looked and to show me how the irons were placed. He seemed familiar with laundries, probably because of the pretty laundresses who ironed the linen. He signed the drawing, "Léon-Poil Fargue," a play on the French word for stove, "*poêle.*"

Adrienne, looking at the glass door, remembered something. Yes, she had seen it before. As a child, she had come with her mother to this very laundry one day. While the women were busy, the little girl had swung on the door, and, of course, smashed the glass. She remembered, too, the spanking she had got when they reached home.

These premises—including the dear old concierge, "la Mère Garrouste," as everyone called her, the kitchenette off the back room, and Adrienne's glass door—everything delighted me, not to mention the very low rent, and I went away to think it over. Mère Garrouste was to think me over, too, for a day or two, according to the best French custom.

Shortly, my mother in Princeton got a cable from me, saying simply: "Opening bookshop in Paris. Please send money," and she sent me all her savings.

Setting Up Shop

It was great fun getting my little shop ready for the book business. I took the advice of my friends the Wright-Worthings, who had the antique shop Aladdin's Lamp in the rue des Saints Pères, and covered the rather damp walls with sackcloth. A humpbacked upholsterer did this for me, and was very proud of the fluting with which he finished off the corners. A carpenter put up shelves and made over the windows for the books to be displayed in, and a painter came to do the few feet of shop front. He called it the "façade," and promised it would be as fine when he finished it as that of the Bazar de l'Hôtel de Ville, his latest triumph. Then a "specialist" came and painted the name "Shakespeare and Company" across the front. That name came to me one night as I lay in bed. My "Partner Bill," as my friend Penny O'Leary called him, was always, I felt, well disposed toward my undertaking; and, besides, he was a best seller.

Charles Winzer, a Polish-English friend of Adrienne's, made the signboard, a portrait of Shakespeare, to be hung outside. Adrienne didn't approve of the idea, but I wanted it anyway. The signboard hung from a bar above the door. I took it down at night. Once, I forgot it, and it was stolen. Winzer made an-

other, which also disappeared. Adrienne's sister made a third
one, a rather French-looking Shakespeare, which I still have.

Now perhaps some people wouldn't know what a "Bookhop" is. Well, that's what the specialist carefully spelled out
above the window at the right, opposite the words "Lending
Library." I let "Bookhop" remain for a while. It quite described
Shakespeare and Company making its debut in bookselling.

All these artisans, in spite of their interest in the place, were
extremely intermittent in their attendance. Sometimes I wondered if they wouldn't still be busy there on the opening day,
upholstering, doing carpentry, and painting the place. At least
the shop, so full of people, would look bustling.

The "office furniture" in my shop was all antique. A charming mirror and a gate-legged table came from the Wright-
Worthings, the rest from the flea market, where you really
found bargains in those days.

The books in my lending library, except for the latest, came
from the well-stocked English secondhand bookstores in Paris.
They, too, were antiques, some of them far too valuable to
be circulated; and if the members of my library hadn't been
so honest, many, instead of a few, of the volumes would soon
have been missing from the shelves. The fascinating bookshop
near the Bourse, Boiveau and Chevillet, which has disappeared
now, was a field of discovery for excavators who were willing
to go down into the cellar, holding a lighted candle provided
by dear old Monsieur Chevillet himself—what a risk!—and
dig up the treasures buried under layers of stuff.

Cyprian, who was in the United States just then, sent me
the latest American books. I went over to London and brought
back two trunks full of English books, mostly poetry. Mrs.
Alida Monro, who with Harold Monro ran the Poetry Bookshop, a wonderful place, very kindly gave me a great deal of
information on the subject of poetry publications and how to
procure them. And I went around to see publishers. All of
them were most courteous and encouraging about the new
bookshop in Paris, and gave me every facility, though, for all

they knew, I might be an adventuress. In fact, so I was.

On the way to the boat train, I stopped in Cork Street at the little bookshop of the publisher and bookseller Elkin Mathews to order my Yeats, Joyce, and Pound. He was sitting in a sort of gallery, with books surging around and creeping up almost to his feet. We had a pleasant talk, and he was quite friendly. I mentioned seeing some drawings by William Blake—if only I could have something of Blake's in my shop! Thereupon he produced two beautiful original drawings, which he sold to me for a sum that, according to Blake experts who saw them later, was absurdly small.

Instead of writing down the titles I wanted from Elkin Mathews—indeed, I hadn't time, and anyway we understood each other so well—I gave him a flying order for Yeats, Joyce, and Pound, and for any portraits he might have of them around the shop. A few days later, in Paris, a huge sack arrived from Elkin Mathews. It contained the works I had ordered, and also dozens of what the French call *"rossignols,"* a poetic name for unsalable items. Obviously, it was a good chance to dump these birds on me. Besides the books, the sack contained some enormous portraits: at least half a dozen of Byron, the rest of Nelson, Wellington, and other characters in English history. Judging by their size, they were intended for the walls of official buildings. I sent them back and scolded Elkin Mathews severely. Still, because of the Blakes, I didn't hold it against him; and I have only pleasant memories of the old gentleman.

Another pleasant memory of my time in London was my visit to the Oxford University Press, where Mr. Humphrey Milford himself showed me the largest Bible in the world, made for Queen Victoria. It wasn't a book you could read in bed.

Shakespeare and Company Opens Its Doors

Instead of setting a date for the opening of my bookshop, I decided that I would simply open it as soon as it was ready.

Finally, the day came when all the books I could afford were on the shelves, and one could walk around the shop without falling over ladders and buckets of paint. Shakespeare and Company opened its doors. The day was November 19, 1919. It had taken me since August to reach this point. In the windows were displayed the works of our Patron, of Chaucer, of T. S. Eliot, Joyce, and so on. There was also Adrienne's favorite English book, *Three Men in a Boat*. Inside, a review rack held copies of the *Nation*, the *New Republic*, the *Dial*, the *New Masses*, *Playboy*, the *Chapbook*, the *Egoist*, the *New English Review*, and other literary magazines. On the walls, I had put up my two Blake drawings, and photographs of Whitman and Poe. Then there were two photographs of Oscar Wilde, in velvet breeches and cloak. They were framed with some of Wilde's letters that a friend of Cyprian's, Byron Kuhn, had given me. Also on display were several little manuscripts of Walt Whitman scribbled on the backs of letters. These were the gift of the poet to my Aunt Agnes Orbison. Aunt Agnes, when she was a student at Bryn Mawr, had gone with her friend Alys Smith to Camden to visit Walt Whitman. (Alys was afterward married to Bertrand Russell, and her sister Mariechen to Bernard Berenson; her brother was Logan Pearsall Smith, who has described some of the doings of this interesting family in his autobiography, *Forgotten Years*.) Alys's mother, Mrs. Hannah Whitall Smith, had given Whitman an armchair, and when Alys and Agnes went to Camden, they didn't find the old man "sitting on a gate," but in the armchair. Manuscripts were strewn over the floor, and some of them, as the shy young Agnes perceived, were in the wastepaper basket. She got up the courage to draw out a few of these scribblings, mostly on the backs of letters addressed to Walt Whitman, Esq., and asked if she might keep them. "Certainly, my dear," he replied. And that's how our family got its Whitman manuscripts.

A good many friends had been waiting for the opening of Shakespeare and Company; and the news soon got around that the time had come. Still, I didn't really expect to see anybody that day. And just as well, I thought. I would need at least twenty-four hours to realize this Shakespeare and Company bookshop. But the shutters in which the little shop went to bed every night were hardly removed (by a waiter from a nearby café) when the first friends began to turn up. From that moment on, for over twenty years, they never gave me time to meditate.

Lending books, just as I had foreseen, was much easier in Paris than selling them. The only cheap editions of English writers were the Tauchnitz and the Conard, and they didn't go much further than Kipling and Hardy in those days. Our moderns, particularly when pounds and dollars were translated into francs, were luxuries the French and my Left Bankers were not able to afford. That is why I was interested in my lending library. So I got everything I liked myself, to share with others in Paris.

My lending library was run on what Adrienne called, though I never knew why, *"le plan américain."* It would have horrified an American librarian, with her catalogues and card indexes and mechanical appliances. It was quite suitable for a library such as mine. There was no catalogue—I preferred to let people find out for themselves how much was lacking; no card index— so unless you could remember, as Adrienne, with her wonderful memory, was able to do, to whom all your books were lent, you had to look through all the members' cards to find out what had become of a volume.

There were, to be sure, the large cards, each bearing the name and address of the member, the date of subscription, the amount of the subscription plus the deposit, and, of course, the title of the book he or she took out. Or books. A member could take one or two volumes, could change them whenever he liked or keep them a fortnight. (Joyce took out dozens, and sometimes kept them for years.) Each member had a small identity card, which he was supposed to produce when claiming the deposit at the expiration of his subscription, or when he was broke. This membership card was as good as a passport, so I was told.

One of the first members of the library was a student at the medical school in the street the rue Dupuytren ran into. This was Thérèse Bertrand, now Dr. Bertrand-Fontaine. I watched her career with excitement. She always passed the exams successfully, went right to the top in her profession, and was appointed *"Médecin des Hôpitaux,"* the first woman to receive that honor. But then, she comes of a family of famous men of science. With all of her work, Thérèse Bertrand found time to read all the new American books in my library, and was a member of it to the day it closed.

The next member (or "bunny," as Holly called them, from the word *abonné:* subscriber) who came along was Gide. I saw Adrienne Monnier coming around the corner from the rue de l'Odéon escorting him. It was just like Gide to hurry up and encourage me in my undertaking. I was always timid in Gide's presence, though Adrienne said, "Pooh!" when I told her; and now, rather overwhelmed by the honor, I wrote on a card: "André Gide: I, Villa Montmorency, Paris XVI; I year; I volume," making a big blot as I did so.

Gide was tall and handsome. He wore a broad-brimmed Stetson, and I saw a resemblance to William S. Hart. He wore either a cape or a sort of Teddy bear coat over his shoulders, and, with his height, he was impressive as he strode along. Gide continued to take an interest in Shakespeare and Company and its proprietor all through the years.

André Maurois was also one of the first to bring me his good wishes. And he brought me a copy of his newly published little masterpiece *Les Silences du Colonel Bramble.*

FOUR

Pilgrims from America

I was too far from my country to follow closely the struggles of the writers there to express themselves, and I didn't foresee, when I opened my bookshop in 1919, that it was going to profit by the suppressions across the sea. I think it was partly to these suppressions, and the atmosphere they created, that I owed many of my customers—all those pilgrims of the twenties who crossed the ocean and settled in Paris and colonized the Left Bank of the Seine.

The news of my bookshop, to my surprise, soon spread all over the United States, and it was the first thing the pilgrims looked up in Paris. They were all customers at Shakespeare and Company, which many of them looked upon as their club. Often, they would inform me that they had given Shakespeare and Company as their address, and they hoped I didn't mind. I didn't, especially since it was too late to do anything about it except to try to run an important mailing office as efficiently as possible.

Every day someone whose work I had seen in the *Little Review* or the *Dial* would appear. Every boat from the other shore brought more customers for Shakespeare and Company.

Of course, prohibition and suppressions were not entirely to blame for the flight of these wild birds from America. The presence in Paris of Joyce and Pound and Picasso and Stravinsky and Everybody—not quite, since T. S. Eliot was in London —had a great deal to do with it.

A good many of my friends camped in Montparnasse, the Saint Germain des Prés of the period. They had only to cross the Luxembourg Gardens.

One of my very first American customers, however, came from Berlin. This was George Antheil, the composer. George and his wife, Böske, walked into the shop, as I remember, one day in 1920, hand in hand. George was stocky in build, had tow-colored bangs, a smashed nose, interesting but wicked-looking eyes, a big mouth and a big grin. He looked like an American high-school boy, of Polish origin, perhaps. Böske, who was Hungarian, was small and pretty and dark-haired, and spoke broken English.

Antheil's ideas interested me, and the fact that he was also from New Jersey was a bond between us. George's father was the proprietor of The Friendly Shoestore in Trenton, next door to Princeton, and now George was about to be my neighbor in Paris. The younger Antheil's interests lay in music rather than in shoes; and at eighteen, all his father's efforts to train a successor having failed, young George had set off for Philadelphia to seek his fortune in music. He was so lucky as to attract the attention of Mrs. Edward Bok. She saw in him a future piano virtuoso, and paid for his tuition. He did become a concert pianist, but in the middle of a tour in Germany he decided that he was more interested in composing than in interpreting other people's compositions, and headed for Paris with his wife, Böske, a student from Budapest whom he had met in Berlin.

Antheil's failure to become a virtuoso was apparently a disappointment to his kind backer, Mrs. Bok. She abandoned him till he could show some proof that his step was justified. George and Böske had to do a good deal of contriving to live on what was left of his earnings from his brief career as a pianist. Böske's

job was to provide goulash for two people with so few pennies.
I entered into all of George's problems.

Often newcomers to Shakespeare and Company were escorted by Robert McAlmon. When did this young poet from
the Middle West come along? Almost as soon as I opened my
bookshop. I shared Bob McAlmon with the Dôme, the Dingo,
and other such places, but his permanent address was c/o Shakespeare and Company, and at least once a day he wandered in.

Robert McAlmon was the youngest child in the large family
of a "nomad pastor," as he described his father, of Scotch-Irish
descent. The only other member of the family I met was
Robert's sister Victoria, whom he liked very much. She went
in for politics, was apparently brilliant, and was running for
something, I forget what.

McAlmon was not tall, and, except for his eyes, which were
a bright blue, not exactly good-looking. Yet, as a rule, he
attracted people, and I knew few who did so as much. Even his
nasal drawl seemed a part of his charm. He was certainly the
most popular member of "the Crowd," as he called it. Somehow, he dominated whatever group he was in. Whatever
café or bar McAlmon patronized at the moment was the one
where you saw everybody. Bob was so busy sharing his interesting ideas with his friends or listening attentively and with
sympathy to their stories of frustration that he neglected his
craft, which was supposed to be writing. All of us who were
interested in Robert McAlmon were looking forward to his
contribution to the writing of the twenties. Unfortunately,
the more he thought of it, the more he was convinced of the
uselessness of effort. "To hell with grammar," he once wrote
to me, "have thrown mine out of the window." He would tell
me he was leaving for the south of France, to look up some
place where he could get away from people and do some
work. I'd get a telegram: "Found right place and quiet room."
Soon somebody would mention seeing Bob down there. "His
room is above the bistrot and they all meet at this bistrot."

My occupation was a daytime one, and a long daytime at that, so I didn't go on to the night clubs with my friends, but the occasional rounds I made were quite bearable with Bob McAlmon in his cups to entertain us.

Mr. and Mrs. Pound

Among the first visitors to my bookshop from across the water —the Channel this time—were Ezra Pound and his wife, Dorothy Shakespear Pound. They had just moved from London, obliged to flee, as Mr. Pound explained to me, because the water was creeping up, and they might wake up some morning to find they had web feet. Mrs. Pound seemed quite unperturbed by this picture of her country. Her mother, I discovered, was the Mrs. Shakespear (without the "e") who had had the famous literary *salon* in England.

Mrs. Pound was afraid people would have difficulty in finding the rue Dupuytren, and I was delighted when she offered to make a little map for the back of the library circular. This map, signed "D. Shakespear," guided many a customer to Shakespeare and Company, and it is among the treasures of those first days of my bookshop.

Mr. Pound looked just as he did in his portraits, the frontispieces in *Lustra* and *Pavannes and Divisions.* His costume— the velvet jacket and the open-road shirt—was that of the English aesthete of the period. There was a touch of Whistler about him; his language, on the other hand, was Huckleberry Finn's.

Mr. Pound was not the kind of writer who talks about his, or, for that matter, anyone's, books; at least with me. I found the acknowledged leader of the modern movement not bumptious. In the course of our conversations, he did boast, but of his carpentry. He asked me if there was anything around the shop that needed mending, and he mended a cigarette box and a chair. I praised his skill, and he invited me to his studio in the rue Notre Dame des Champs to see his furniture, all made by himself. He had painted all the woodwork, too.

Joyce, commenting on Pound's furniture, thought a cobbler should stick to his last, but I'm sure a *"violon d'Ingres"* is a very good thing for a writer. I learned with interest from Catherine Carswell's book that when D. H. Lawrence washed the pots and pans, the tea towels that dried them always remained clean, and from Dorothy Brett that when he was in Mexico, he painted the water closet a bright color and decorated it with a phoenix.

I saw Mr. Pound seldom. He was busy with his work and his young poets; his music, too. He and George Antheil were cooking up plans to revolutionize music.

Two Customers from the Rue de Fleurus

Not long after I had opened my bookshop, two women came walking down the rue Dupuytren. One of them, with a very fine face, was stout, wore a long robe, and, on her head, a most becoming top of a basket. She was accompanied by a slim, dark whimsical woman: she reminded me of a gipsy. They were Gertrude Stein and Alice B. Toklas.

Having been an early reader of *Tender Buttons* and *Three Lives*, I was, of course, very joyful over my new customers. And I enjoyed their continual banter. Gertrude was always teasing me about my bookselling, which appeared to amuse her considerably. It amused me, too.

Her remarks and those of Alice, which rounded them out, were inseparable. Obviously they saw things from the same angle, as people do when they are perfectly congenial. Their two characters, however, seemed to me quite independent of each other. Alice had a great deal more finesse than Gertrude. And she was grown up: Gertrude was a child, something of an infant prodigy.

Gertrude subscribed to my lending library, but complained

that there were no amusing books in it. Where, she asked in-
dignantly, were those American masterpieces *The Trail of the
Lonesome Pine* and *The Girl of the Limberlost?* This was
humiliating for the librarian. I produced the works of Gertrude
Stein, all I had been able to lay my hands on at the time, and
I wondered if she could mention another library in Paris that
had two copies of *Tender Buttons* circulating. To make up for
her unjust criticism of Shakespeare and Company, she bestowed
several of her works on us: quite rare items such as *Portrait of
Mabel Dodge at the Villa Curonia* and that thing with the
terrifying title, *Have They Attacked Mary: He giggled: A
Political Caricature.* Also the special number of the Stieglitz
publication, *Camera Work*, containing her pieces on Picasso
and Matisse. But, above all, I valued the copy of *Melanctha* in
the first edition, which Gertrude inscribed for me. I should
have locked it up; someone stole it from the bookshop.

Gertrude's subscription was merely a friendly gesture. She
took little interest, of course, in any but her own books. But
she did write a poem about my bookshop, which she brought
to me one day in 1920. It was entitled "Rich and Poor in
English" and bore the subtitle, "to subscribe in French and
other Latin Tongues." You can find it in *Painted Lace*, Volume
V of the Yale edition of her work.

I saw Gertrude and Alice often. Either they dropped in to
observe my bookselling business or I went around to their
pavillon in the rue de Fleurus near the Luxembourg Gardens.
It was at the back of the court. Gertrude always lay stretched
on a divan and always joked and teased. The *pavillon* was as
fascinating as its occupants. On its walls were all those wonderful Picassos of the "Blue period." Also, Gertrude showed me
the albums that contained his drawings, of which she had collected a good many. She told me that she and her brother, Leo,
had agreed to divide between them all the pictures they possessed. He had chosen Matisse, she Picasso. I remember some
paintings by Juan Gris, too.

Once, Gertrude and Alice took me for a ride into the country. They drove up noisily in the old Ford named Gody, a veteran of the war and companion in their war work. Gertrude showed me Gody's latest acquisition—headlights that could be turned on and off at will from inside the car and an electric cigarette lighter. Gertrude smoked continuously. I climbed up on the high seat beside Gertrude and Alice, and off we roared to Mildred Aldrich's "hilltop on the Marne." Gertrude did the driving, and presently, when a tire blew out, she did the mending. Very competently too, while Alice and I chatted by the roadside.

Gertrude Stein's admirers, until they had met her and discovered how affable she was, were often "skeered" to approach her without proper protection. So the poor things would come to me, exactly as if I were a guide from one of the tourist agencies, and beg me to take them to see Gertrude Stein.

My tours, arranged with Gertrude and Alice beforehand, took place in the evenings. They were cheerfully endured by the ladies in the *pavillon*, who were always cordial and hospitable.

One of the first of these tourists was a young friend of mine who hung around Shakespeare and Company a great deal in 1919-20, Stephen Benét. He may be seen in one of the first press photos of the bookshop, that fellow peering through his glasses at a book and very serious-looking compared with my sister Holly and me in the back of the shop.

At his request, and on his own responsibility, I took Stephen to see Gertrude Stein. This was before his marriage to that charming Rosemary, whom he later brought to the bookshop. The visit to Gertrude went off pleasantly. I believe Stephen mentioned that he had some Spanish blood, and since Gertrude and Alice liked anything Spanish, that interested them. I don't think the meeting left any traces, however.

Sherwood Anderson

Another "tourist" who asked me to take him around to the rue de Fleurus was Sherwood Anderson. One day I noticed an interesting-looking man lingering on the doorstep, his eye caught by a book in the window. The book was *Winesburg, Ohio*, which had recently been published in the United States. Presently he came in and introduced himself as the author. He said he hadn't seen another copy of his book in Paris. I was not surprised, as I had looked everywhere for it myself—in one place they had said, "Anderson, Anderson? Oh, sorry, we have only the Fairy Tales."

Sherwood Anderson was full of something that had happened to him, a step he had taken, a decision he had made that was of the greatest importance in his life. I listened with suspense to the story of how he had suddenly abandoned his home and a prosperous paint business, had simply walked away one morning, shaking off forever the fetters of respectability and the burden of security.

Anderson was a man of great charm, and I became very fond of him. I saw him as a mixture of poet and evangelist (without the preaching), with perhaps a touch of the actor. Anyhow, he was a most interesting man.

I knew Adrienne would like Sherwood Anderson and that he would like her, so I took him to her bookshop, and she was indeed struck by him. He was immediately invited to supper. Adrienne cooked a chicken, her specialty, and both chicken and cook made a big hit. Anderson and Adrienne got on very well together, she speaking pidgin American, he pidgin French. They discovered that there was a great similarity of ideas between them. In spite of the language barrier, Adrienne understood Sherwood better than I did. Describing him to me afterward, she said he resembled an old woman, an Indian squaw, smoking her pipe at the fireside. Adrienne had seen squaws at Buffalo Bill's show in Paris.

When Anderson first came to Paris, he asked me, since he didn't speak French, to go with him to the Nouvelle Revue Française, his French publishers. He wanted to find out what had become of his works. After a rather long wait to be admitted to the editor's office, Sherwood got angry and threatened to break up the whole place. It looked for a moment as if we were going to have a regular Western. Then, fortunately, doors opened, and we were invited inside.

Sherwood told me that Gertrude Stein's writing had influenced him. He admired her immensely, and asked me if I would introduce him to her. I knew he needed no introduction, but I gladly consented to conduct him to the rue de Fleurus.

This meeting was something of an event. Sherwood's deference and the admiration he expressed for her writing pleased Gertrude immensely. She was visibly touched. Sherwood's wife, Tennessee, who had accompanied us, didn't fare so well. She tried in vain to take part in the interesting conversation between the two writers, but Alice held her off. I knew the rules and regulations about wives at Gertrude's. They couldn't be kept from coming, but Alice had strict orders to keep them out of the way while Gertrude conversed with the husbands. Tennessee was less tractable than most. She seated herself on a table ready to take part in the conversation, and resisted when Alice offered to show her something on the other side of the sitting room. But Tennessee never succeeded in hearing a word of what they were saying. I pitied the thwarted lady—I couldn't see the necessity for the cruelty to wives that was practiced in the rue de Fleurus. Still, I couldn't help being amused at Alice's wife-proof technique. Curiously, it was only applied to wives; non-wives were admitted to Gertrude's conversation.

Sherwood Anderson was judged harshly by the young writers; and suffered considerably from the falling-off of his followers. But he was a forerunner, and, whether they acknowledge it or not, the generation of the twenties owes him a considerable debt.

Gertrude Stein had so much charm that she could often, though not always, get away with the most monstrous absurdities, which she uttered with a certain childish malice. Her aim was usually to tease somebody; nothing amused her as much. Adrienne Monnier, whom I took around to Gertrude's once, didn't find her very amusing. "You French," Gertrude declared, "have no Alps in literature, no Shakespeare; all your genius is in those speeches of the generals: fanfare. Such as 'On ne passera pas!' "

I disagreed with Gertrude on French writing as well as on other writing, for instance, Joyce's. She was disappointed in me when I published *Ulysses;* she even came with Alice to my bookshop to announce that they had transferred their membership to the American Library on the Right Bank. I was sorry, of course, to lose two customers all of a sudden, but one mustn't coerce them. In the rue de l'Odéon, I must admit, we kept low company.

Thus "The Flowers of Friendship Faded Friendship Faded," at least for a time. But resentment fades as well. It's so difficult to remember exactly what a disagreement was all about. And there was Gertrude Stein's writing; nothing could affect my enjoyment of that.

After a while, I saw Gertrude and Alice again. They came to see whether I had anything by William Dean Howells, a major American writer, according to Gertrude, and unjustly neglected. I had his complete works, and made Gertrude and Alice take them all home.

Toward the end of 1930, I went one day with Joyce to a party at the studio of our friend Jo Davidson. Gertrude Stein, a fellow-bust of Joyce's, was also there. They had never met, so, with their mutual consent, I introduced them to each other and saw them shake hands quite peacefully.

Dear Jo Davidson! How we did miss him when he was gone.

The last time I took a "skeered" person to see Gertrude was when Ernest Hemingway told me he wanted to make up his quarrel with her but couldn't get up the courage to go alone. I encouraged him in his plan, and promised to accompany him to the rue Christine, where Gertrude and Alice were then living. I thought it better for Hemingway to go up alone, so I took him all the way to her door and left him with my best wishes. He came to tell me afterward that it was "fine" between them again.

Wars between writers blaze up frequently, but I have observed that they settle down eventually into smudges.

FIVE

Ulysses in Paris

It was in the summer of 1920, when my bookshop was in its first year, that I met James Joyce.

One sultry Sunday afternoon, Adrienne was going to a party at André Spire's. She insisted on my accompanying her, assuring me that the Spires would be delighted, but I hung back. Though I admired Spire's poetry, I didn't know him personally. Finally, Adrienne had her way, as usual, and we set off together to Neuilly, where the Spires were living at the time.

They had an apartment on the second floor of a house at 34 rue du Bois de Boulogne; I remember the shady trees around it. Spire, rather Blake-like with his Biblical beard and curly mane, greeted his uninvited guest with great cordiality, and presently, drawing me aside, whispered in my ear, "The Irish writer James Joyce is here."

I worshiped James Joyce, and on hearing the unexpected news that he was present, I was so frightened I wanted to run away, but Spire told me it was the Pounds who had brought the Joyces—we could see Ezra through the open door. I knew the Pounds, so I went in.

There, indeed, was Ezra, stretched out in a big armchair. According to an article of mine in the *Mercure de France*,

34

Pound was wearing a becoming blue shirt matching his eyes, but he wrote to me immediately to say that he had never had blue eyes at all. So I take back the blue eyes.

I saw Mrs. Pound, and I went over to speak to her. She was talking to an attractive young woman whom she introduced as Mrs. Joyce; and then she left us together.

Mrs. Joyce was rather tall, and neither stout nor thin. She was charming, with her reddish curly hair and eyelashes, her eyes with a twinkle in them, her voice with its Irish inflections, and a certain dignity that is so Irish also. She seemed glad to find that we could speak English together. She couldn't understand a word of what was being said. Now if it had been Italian! The Joyces had lived in Trieste. They all knew Italian, and even spoke it at home.

Our conversation was interrupted when Spire invited us all to sit down at a long table set out with a delicious cold supper. As we ate and drank, I noticed one guest who was not drinking at all. He resisted Spire's repeated efforts to fill his glass; finally, he turned his glass upside down, and that settled it. The guest was James Joyce. He got very red when Pound began to line up all the bottles on the table in front of his plate.

His father was an alcoholic

After supper, Adrienne Monnier and Julien Benda began a discussion of Benda's recently expressed views on the top writers of the period. A group of interested listeners gathered around, balancing their coffee cups. Benda's attack was directed against Valéry, Gide, Claudel, and others.

Leaving Adrienne to defend her friends, I strolled into a little room lined to the ceiling with books. There, drooping in a corner between two bookcases, was Joyce.

Trembling, I asked: "Is this the great James Joyce?"

"James Joyce," he replied.

We shook hands; that is, he put his limp, boneless hand in my tough little paw—if you can call that a handshake.

He was of medium height, thin, slightly stooped, graceful. One noticed his hands. They were very narrow. On the middle and third fingers of the left hand, he wore rings, the stones in heavy settings. His eyes, a deep blue, with the light of genius in them, were extremely beautiful. I noticed, however, that the right eye had a slightly abnormal look and that the right lens of his glasses was thicker than the left. His hair was thick, sandy-colored, wavy, and brushed back from a high, lined forehead over his tall head. He gave an impression of sensitiveness exceeding any I had ever known. His skin was fair, with a few freckles, and rather flushed. On his chin was a sort of goatee. His nose was well-shaped, his lips narrow and fine-cut. I thought he must have been very handsome as a young man.

Joyce's voice, with its sweet tones pitched like a tenor's, charmed me. His enunciation was exceptionally clear. His pronunciation of certain words such as "book" (bōo-k) and "look" (lōo-k) and those beginning with "th" was Irish, and the voice particularly was Irish. Otherwise there was nothing to distinguish his English from that of the Englishman. He expressed himself quite simply but, as I observed, with a care for the words and the sounds—partly, no doubt, because of his love of language and his musical ear, but also, I believe, because he had spent so many years teaching English.

Joyce told me that he had arrived only recently in Paris. Ezra Pound had suggested his moving there with his family. Through Pound, Joyce had met Madame Ludmilla Savitzky, and she had turned over her flat in Passy to the Joyces for a few weeks, giving them time to look for a place of their own. Madame Savitzky was one of Joyce's first friends in Paris and translated *A Portrait of the Artist as a Young Man* (*Dédalus* was its French title). Another early friend in Paris was Mrs. Jenny Bradley, who translated *Exiles*.

"What do you do?" Joyce inquired. I told him about Shakespeare and Company. The name, and mine, too, seemed to amuse him, and a charming smile came to his lips. Taking a small notebook out of his pocket and, as I noticed with sadness, holding it very close to his eyes, he wrote down the name and address. He said he would come to see me.

Suddenly a dog barked, and Joyce turned pale; he actually trembled. The bark came from across the road. I looked out of the window and saw a dog running after a ball. It had a loud bark but, as far as I could tell, no bite.

"Is it coming in? Is it fierce?" Joyce asked me, very uneasy. (He pronounced it "feerrce.") I assured him it wasn't coming in, and didn't look at all fierce, but he was still apprehensive and startled by every bark. He told me he had been afraid of dogs since the age of five, when one of "the animals" had bitten him on the chin. Pointing to his goatee, he said that it was to hide the scar.

We talked on. Joyce's manner was so extremely simple that, overcome though I was in the presence of the greatest writer of my time, I somehow felt at ease with him. This first time, and afterward, I was always conscious of his genius, yet I knew no one so easy to talk with.

Now the guests were leaving, and Adrienne was looking for me to say good-by to the Spires. As I thanked Spire for his hospitality, he said he hoped I hadn't been bored. Bored? I had met James Joyce.

The very next day, Joyce came walking up my steep little street wearing a dark blue serge suit, a black felt hat on the back of his head, and, on his narrow feet, not so very white sneakers. He was twirling a cane, and, when he saw me looking at it, he told me that it was an ashplant stick from Ireland, the gift of an Irish officer on a British man-of-war that had stopped at the Port of Trieste. ("Stephen Dedalus," I thought, "still has his ashplant.") Joyce was always a bit shabby, but his bearing was so graceful and his manner so distinguished that one scarcely noticed what he had on. Everywhere he went and on everyone he met, he made a deep impression.

He stepped into my bookshop, peered closely at the photographs of Walt Whitman and Edgar Allan Poe, then at the two Blake drawings; finally, he inspected my two photographs of

Oscar Wilde. Then he sat down in the uncomfortable little armchair beside my table.

He told me again that Pound had persuaded him to come to Paris. Now he had three problems: finding a roof to put over the heads of four people; feeding and clothing them; and finishing *Ulysses*. The first problem was the most urgent. Madame Savitzky was going to give up her apartment in two weeks, and then he must find another one for his family.

And there was the financial problem. He had spent his entire savings on the removal to Paris. He must look for pupils. If I heard of people wanting lessons, would I send them to Professor Joyce? He had had a great deal of experience, he said. In Trieste, he had taught for years at the Berlitz School and had also given private lessons; in Zurich, too, he had taught. "What languages did you teach?" I asked. "English," he said. " 'This is the table. This is the pen.' Also German, Latin, even French." "And Greek?" I asked. He knew no old Greek; modern Greek he spoke fluently—he had picked it up from the Greek sailors in Trieste.

Languages apparently were Joyce's favorite sport. I asked him how many he knew. There were at least nine; we counted them. Besides his own, he spoke Italian, French, German, Greek, Spanish, Dutch, and the three Scandinavian tongues. He had learned Norwegian in order to read Ibsen, and had followed it with Swedish and Danish. He also spoke Yiddish, knew Hebrew. He didn't mention Chinese and Japanese. He probably left them to Pound.

He told me how he had got out of Trieste when the war came. It had been a narrow escape. The Austrians were about to arrest him as a spy, but a friend, Baron Ralli, obtained a visa just in time for him to get his family out of the country. They had managed to reach Zurich, and had stayed there till the end of the war.

I wondered when Joyce found time to write. At night, he said, after the lessons were over. He was beginning to feel the strain on his eyes. He had begun to have trouble with them by the time he went to Zurich, and there it had become serious— glaucoma. It was the first time I had ever heard of this disease, with its beautiful name. "The gray owl eyes of Athena," said Joyce.

He had had an operation on the right eye; perhaps I had noticed the thick lens over it. He described the operation simply (he was accustomed, I observed, to explaining things to backward pupils like me); he even made a little drawing to make it clear to me. In his opinion it had been a mistake to operate in the middle of an attack of iritis. As a consequence, he thought, the sight in that eye had been impaired.

With this eye trouble, wasn't it difficult for him to write? Did he sometimes dictate? "Never!" he exclaimed. He always wrote by hand. He liked to be held back, would otherwise go too fast. He had to see his work as he shaped it word by word.

I had been longing to hear about *Ulysses*. Now I inquired whether he was progressing in it. "I am." (An Irishman never says "yes.") He had been working on the book for seven years and was trying to finish it. He would go on with it as soon as he got settled in Paris.

It appeared that Mr. John Quinn, the brilliant Irish-American lawyer in New York, was buying the manuscript of *Ulysses* bit by bit. As soon as Joyce completed an instalment, he made a fair copy and sent it off to Quinn, who, in return, sent Joyce the sum agreed on—small sums, but they helped.

I mentioned the *Little Review*: Had Margaret Anderson succeeded in her efforts to publish *Ulysses*? Had there been more suppressions? Joyce looked anxious. The news from New York was alarming. He would keep me informed, he said.

Before he went away he asked how he could become a member of my lending library. Taking *Riders to the Sea* from the shelf, he said he would like to borrow it. He had once translated the play into German, he said, for performance by a little theatrical group he had organized in Zurich.

I wrote down: "James Joyce: 5, rue de l'Assomption, Paris; subscription for one month; seven francs." And we said good-by.

I was deeply moved to learn from Joyce himself of the circumstances in which he had been working all these years.

James Joyce, Care of Shakespeare and Company

Joyce was now a member of the family of Shakespeare and Company, its most illustrious member. He was often to be seen in the bookshop. He obviously enjoyed the company of my compatriots. He confided to me that he liked us and our language; certainly he made plenty of use of the American vernacular in his books.

At the bookshop he met many young writers who became friends of his: Robert McAlmon, William Bird, Ernest Hemingway, Archibald MacLeish, Scott Fitzgerald—and also the composer George Antheil. Joyce was, of course, their god, but their manner toward him was one of friendliness rather than of veneration.

As for Joyce, he treated people invariably as his equals, whether they were writers, children, waiters, princesses, or charladies. What anybody had to say interested him; he told me that he had never met a bore. Sometimes I would find him waiting for me at the bookshop, listening attentively to a long tale my concierge was telling him. If he arrived in a taxi, he wouldn't get out until the driver had finished what he was saying. Joyce himself fascinated everybody; no one could resist his charm.

I loved to see Joyce walking up the street twirling his ashplant stick, his hat on the back of his head. "Melancholy Jesus," Adrienne and I used to call him. It was from Joyce himself that I learned this expression. Also "Crooked Jesus" (he pronounced it "crōo-ked").

He had a way of wrinkling up his face that amused me—

it looked rather simian at such times. As for his way of sitting, I can only describe it as "broken up."

Joyce used to exclaim frequently (his daughter's name for him was "l'Esclammadore") but his language was always mild; never a swearword or the slightest coarseness. His favorite ejaculation was the Italian "*Già!*" He sighed a great deal.

His manner of expressing himself was unemphatic; he had no use for superlatives. Even the worst happenings he described as "tiresome." Not even "very tiresome," just "tiresome." I think he disliked the word "very." "Why say 'very beautiful'?" I once heard him complain. " 'Beautiful' is enough."

He was invariably courteous and extremely considerate of others. My rough-and-tumble compatriots used to come and go without greeting anybody, as if my bookshop were a railway station, or if they did hail somebody, it was "Hi Hem" or "Hi Bob." In this informal atmosphere, Joyce alone was formal—excessively so. It is a custom in the French literary world to address writers by their last names. In spite of Monsieur Teste or Monsieur Charlus, you would never think of calling their authors "Monsieur Valéry" or "Monsieur Proust." If you were a disciple, you addressed them as "Maître." Valéry always called Adrienne "Monnier" and myself "Sylvia" as all our other French friends did. I know this custom shocked Joyce. In vain did he set a good example by his "Miss Monnier" and "Miss Beach." But let no one dare to call him anything but "Mr. Joyce"!

"Mr. Joyce" was also rather quaint when it came to the mention of certain things in the presence of ladies. He blushed scarlet over the stories that Léon-Paul Fargue used to tell to mixed audiences at Adrienne's bookshop. The ladies themselves, in a country where the men don't get off by themselves, were not at all disturbed. I'm sure Joyce regretted that his nice lady editress should be exposed to such things, but I fear I had become inured by many a Fargue session.

Yet Joyce had no objection to putting *Ulysses* into the hands of ladies, or to ladies publishing it.

Joyce came to the bookshop every day, but I had to go to their home to see the rest of the family. I was very fond of them all: Georgio, with his gruffness, hiding or trying to hide his feelings; Lucia, the humorous one—neither of them happy in the strange circumstances in which they grew up; and Nora, the wife and mother, who scolded them all, including her husband, for their shiftlessness. Joyce enjoyed being called a good-for-nothing by Nora; it was a relief from the respectful attitude of others. He was delighted when she poked and pushed him.

Nora would have no truck with books, and that, too, amused her husband. She declared to me that she hadn't read a page of "that book," pointing to *Ulysses*; nothing would induce her to open it. I could see myself that it was quite unnecessary for Nora to read *Ulysses*; was she not the source of his inspiration?

Nora grumbled about "my husband"; he never stopped scribbling . . . reaching down when he was only half awake in the morning for his paper and pencil on the floor beside him . . . never knowing what time of day it was! And how could she keep a servant if he left the house just at the moment when she was putting lunch on the table? "Look at him now! Leeching on the bed, and scribbling away!" The children, too; they wouldn't lift a finger to help her, she said. "A good-for-nothing family!" Whereupon the whole good-for-nothing lot of them, including Joyce, would burst out laughing. Nobody seemed to take Nora's scoldings very seriously.

She used to tell me that she was sorry she hadn't married a farmer or a banker, or maybe a ragpicker, instead of a writer— her lips curled as she mentioned this despicable kind of person. But what a good thing for Joyce, I thought, that she had chosen him. What would he have done without Nora? And what would his work have done without her? His marriage to Nora was one of the best pieces of luck that ever befell him. His was certainly the happiest marriage of any writer I knew.

Joyce's effort to be a good family man and respectable burgher, "Burjoice," Sherwood Anderson called it, was touch-

ing. It didn't fit the "Artist" of the *Portrait*. But it helped you
to understand *Ulysses*. It is so interesting to see how Stephen
recedes and grows dimmer, while Bloom emerges and stands
out clearer and clearer, finally taking over the whole show. I
felt that Joyce fast lost interest in Stephen and that it was Mr.
Bloom who had come between them. After all, there was a
good deal of Bloom in Joyce.

Joyce's fear of a great many things was real, though I think
it was partly cultivated as a counterbalance to his fearlessness
where his art was concerned. He seemed afraid of "catching it"
from God Almighty. The Jesuits must have succeeded in
putting the fear of God into him. I have seen Joyce, when a
thunderstorm was going on, cower in the hall of his apartment
till it was over. He was afraid of heights, of the sea, of infection.
Then there were his superstitions, which were shared by the
family. Seeing two nuns in the street was bad luck (a taxi he
was in collided with another vehicle on one of these occasions);
numbers and dates were lucky or unlucky. Opening an umbrella in the house, a man's hat on the bed were ill omens.
Black cats, on the contrary, were lucky. Arriving one day at the
Joyces' hotel, I saw Nora trying to induce a black cat to go
into the room where her husband was lying, while through the
open door he anxiously observed her efforts. Cats were not only
lucky, Joyce liked having them about, and once, when a
kitten of his daughter's fell out of the kitchen window, he was
as upset about it as she was.

Dogs, on the contrary, he always suspected of being fierce.
I used to have to hurry a harmless little white one of mine out
of the shop before Joyce would come in. It was useless to remind him of his Odyssean hero, whose faithful dog Argos
dropped dead of joy over his master's home-coming. Joyce
only exclaimed "*Già!*" with a laugh.

Joyce, with his patriarchal ideas, regretted that he hadn't ten
children. He was devoted to the two he had, and was never too
much absorbed in his own work to encourage them in theirs.
He was very proud of Georgio, or "Georgy," as his mother

called him, and of his fine voice. The Joyces were all singers, and Joyce never quite ceased to regret his choice of a writer's instead of a singer's career. "Perhaps I would have done better," he would say to me. "Maybe," I would reply, "but you have done pretty well as a writer."

SIX

Shakespeare and Company to the Rescue

Joyce's chief concern at this time was the fate of *Ulysses*. It was still appearing, or trying to appear, in the *Little Review*, but the future looked dark for both the book and the magazine.

In England, Miss Harriet Weaver had already fought and lost her battle of *Ulysses*. It was Miss Weaver, pioneer Joycean, who had published in her review, the *Egoist*, *A Portrait of the Artist*, which first gained recognition for the new Irish writer James Joyce. He had been discovered by Ezra Pound, a great showman and the leader of a gang that hung out around the *Egoist* and included such suspicious characters as Richard Aldington, H. D., T. S. Eliot, Wyndham Lewis, and others almost as bad.

A Portrait of the Artist made a great impression in England. Even H. G. Wells came out in praise of it, and Miss Weaver intended to give her subscribers "Mr. Joyce's" second novel, *Ulysses*. Five instalments did appear in the *Egoist* in 1919. It went no further than the episode of the Wandering Rocks. Miss Weaver was having printing troubles and, besides, she was getting letters from subscribers complaining that *Ulysses* wasn't suitable for a periodical that had its place on the table in the living room with the family reading matter. Some of them even went so far as to cancel their subscriptions.

Since there were objections to publishing *Ulysses* in a periodical, Miss Weaver, rather than give in, sacrificed the review. The *Egoist* review turned into the Egoist Press, "overnight," as she expressed it. Her sole object in making this move was to publish James Joyce's entire works. She announced the "forthcoming publication of *Ulysses*," but she was unable to carry out her plans.

Miss Weaver attempted to bring out *A Portrait of the Artist* in book form, but was unable to find a printer who would set it up, English printers being extremely wary of Joyce's name. She made an arrangement with Mr. Huebsch, Joyce's publisher in New York, whereby he sent her sheets of his edition which were then issued under the Egoist imprint.

Miss Weaver explained to me why English printers are so finicky. Their prudence is indeed quite excusable. If a book is found objectionable by the authorities, the printer as well as the publisher is held responsible and must pay the penalty. No wonder he scrutinizes every little word that might get him into trouble. Joyce once showed me the proofs of Mr. Jonathan Cape's new printing of *A Portrait of the Artist*, and I remember my amazement at the printer's queries in the margins.

Miss Weaver saw that the difficulties would be too great if she persisted in her efforts to bring out *Ulysses*, and she saw no hope, at least for the present, of succeeding in doing so. Moreover, she was warned by her friends that she would only let herself in for a lot of unpleasantness. So *Ulysses* had wandered overseas to the *Little Review*; and was again in trouble.

A big fight was going on between the *Little Review* and the American authorities. Joyce brought me disturbing news from the battlefield.

Three seizures of the magazine by officials of the United States Post Office, on the grounds of obscenity, failed to break the spirit of the editors, Margaret Anderson and Jane Heap;

but a fourth one, which was instigated by John S. Sumner of the Society for the Suppression of Vice, put an end to the magazine. Eventually, Miss Anderson and Miss Heap were tried for the publication of obscenity. Thanks to the brilliant defense of John Quinn, they got off with a fine of one hundred dollars, but by that time they were ruined financially. Sad was the disappearance of the liveliest little magazine of the period!

Joyce came to announce the news. It was a heavy blow for him, and I felt, too, that his pride was hurt. In a tone of complete discouragement, he said, "My book will never come out now."

All hope of publication in the English-speaking countries, at least for a long time to come, was gone. And here in my little bookshop sat James Joyce, sighing deeply.

It occurred to me that something might be done, and I asked: "Would you let Shakespeare and Company have the honor of bringing out your *Ulysses*?"

He accepted my offer immediately and joyfully. I thought it rash of him to entrust his great *Ulysses* to such a funny little publisher. But he seemed delighted, and so was I. We parted, both of us, I think, very much moved. He was to come back next day to hear what Adrienne Monnier, "Shakespeare and Company's Adviser," as Joyce called her, thought of my plan. I always consulted her before taking an important step. She was such a wise counselor, and she was, besides, a sort of partner in the firm.

Adrienne thoroughly approved of my idea. She had heard a great deal about Joyce from me, and I had no trouble convincing her of the importance of rescuing *Ulysses*.

When Joyce came back the next day, I was glad to see him so cheerful. As for me, imagine how happy I was to find myself suddenly the publisher of the work I admired above all. I was lucky, I thought.

Undeterred by lack of capital, experience, and all the other requisites of a publisher, I went right ahead with *Ulysses*.

Darantiere of Dijon

Adrienne Monnier's printer, Monsieur Maurice Darantiere, came to see me. He and his father before him were "Master Printers." The works of Huysmans and many another writer of the same period had been printed by Darantiere in Dijon.

Darantiere was much interested in what I told him about the banning of *Ulysses* in the English-speaking countries. I announced my intention of bringing out this work in France, and asked him if he would print it. At the same time, I laid bare my financial situation, and warned him that there could be no question of paying for the printing till the money from the subscriptions came in—if it did come in. The work would have to be done with that understanding.

M. Darantiere agreed to take on the printing of *Ulysses* on these terms. Very friendly and sporting of him, I must say!

Joyce was now haunting the bookshop to keep in touch with events step by step. I asked him for suggestions, and usually took them. But not always; for instance, he thought that if a dozen or so copies were printed there would be some left over. A thousand copies were to be printed, I told him firmly. (There were none left over.)

A prospectus was printed announcing that *Ulysses*, by James Joyce, would be published "complete as written" (a most important point) by Shakespeare and Company, Paris, in "the autumn of 1921." The prospectus stated that the edition was to be limited to a thousand copies: one hundred printed on Dutch paper and signed, at 350 francs; one hundred and fifty on vergé-d'Arches, at 250 francs; and the remaining seven hundred and fifty on ordinary paper, at 150 francs. There was a postage-stamp-sized photo of the author, gaunt and bearded—the one taken in Zurich—and excerpts from articles by those critics who had spotted *Ulysses* on its first appearance in the *Little Review*. On the back of the prospectus was a blank form to be filled in with the subscriber's name and his choice of the kind of copy he wanted. Adrienne, who had done some publishing herself, initiated me into the mysteries of limited editions, on the subject of which I was totally ignorant. It was thanks to her also that my prospectus was professional-looking; you might have thought I was an experienced hand at this sort of thing. Monsieur Darantiere brought me samples of his finest paper and a specimen of his famous type, and I learned for the first time the rules that govern de luxe editions.

As yet I was only in the apprentice stage of bookselling. I had the lending library, too, and the place was swirling with young writers and their budding enterprises. Now suddenly I found myself a publisher as well, and of what a book! It was time to look around for an assistant. A charming Greek girl, Mademoiselle Myrsine Moschos, a member of the library, said that she would like to help me. The job would be ill-paid, and I did my best to dissuade Mlle. Moschos from accepting it, pointing out that she could do much better for herself in something else, but she had made up her mind and still wanted to come, luckily for Shakespeare and Company.

Joyce was delighted to hear of my Greek assistant. He thought it a good omen for his *Ulysses*. Omen or no omen, I was delighted to have someone to help me now, and someone who was a wonderful helper. Myrsine worked side by side with me for nine years. She was invaluable as an assistant, as interested as I in everything going on, not afraid of manual work, of which there is a great deal to be done in a bookshop, or of the still harder and more delicate job of dealing with the customers and understanding the needs of the members of the library, which required a lot of understanding.

One of Myrsine's great assets was her large family of sisters, on whom we could always fall back in time of need. Hélène, the youngest of the Moschos daughters, acted as messenger between Joyce and the bookshop. She would set off in the morning with a brief case stuffed with mail, books, theatre tickets, and other things, and return with a load just as heavy. Joyce awaited what he called her "t'undering step"—she had rather a heavy step for such a small person. When all her messenger business was done, he would perhaps detain her to read something in a magazine aloud to him, and he was probably more interested in Hélène's pronunciation, for instance, of "*Doublevé Vé Yats*" (W. B. Yeats), than in the article itself.

Myrsine's father, Dr. Moschos, was a nomadic medical man. He had wandered almost as much as Odysseus, and had had nine children in as many countries. Dr. Moschos introduced to me a man who had outdone Ulysses in cunning, but whose cunning had turned out to be somewhat of a boomerang. This man was stone deaf, but had not always been so. To evade the draft when he came up for military service, he pretended to be deaf. He was exempted, but to be safe he kept up his deafness for some time. Then, when it was no longer necessary to continue his strategy, he found he had completely lost his hearing, and for good. I don't know whether this astounding case was ever reported to learned bodies, or whether or not an ear specialist would believe it, but it is true.

Myrsine had a good many friends from oriental countries. Among these was a young prince, heir to the throne of Cambodia and a student at the Medical School in Paris. This young man changed his name from Ritarasi to Ulysses in honor of Joyce's masterpiece.

A Missing Subscriber

Subscriptions for *Ulysses* began coming in fast, and were piled up according to their nationality. All of my customers and many of Adrienne's were among them; nobody escaped from the rue de l'Odéon without subscribing. Some of Adrienne's French friends amused me very much when they admitted that their English vocabulary was limited but that they were pinning their hopes on *Ulysses* to enlarge it. Even André Gide, the first of our French friends to rush to my bookshop and fill in one of the subscription blanks, must have had some difficulty in reading *Ulysses*, though he always carried some English book or other in his pocket. I'm sure, however, that Gide came immediately not so much to subscribe for *Ulysses* as to show a friendly interest, as he always did, in any of our rue de l'Odéon enterprises. He was always sure to give his support to the cause of freedom of expression, whenever the occasion arose. Gide's gesture none the less surprised me, and I thought it very touching. Adrienne said it was characteristic of him.

Ezra Pound made a sensation when he deposited on my table one day a subscription blank with the signature of W. B. Yeats on it. Ernest Hemingway was down for several copies of the book.

Then we had Robert McAlmon, who was untiring. He combed the night clubs for subscribers, and every morning, early, on his way home, left another "Hasty Bunch" of the signed forms, the signatures slightly zigzag, some of them. When *Ulysses* came out, I met people who were surprised to find themselves subscribers, but they always took it cheerfully when McAlmon explained it to them.

As time went on, I began to wonder why Bernard Shaw's name was not on the list of subscribers for *Ulysses*. There were two reasons why I thought Shaw would subscribe: first, the revolutionary aspect of *Ulysses* should appeal to him; and, second, knowing Joyce's circumstances, as he certainly couldn't help doing, he would want to come to the help of a fellow writer with a contribution in the shape of a subscription. I had reason to think that, in such matters, Shaw was kind; Mrs. Desmond Fitzgerald, who had been his secretary for a time, told me that his generosity when appealed to was extraordinary, but that he kept it very quiet.

I told Joyce that I intended to send a prospectus to Shaw, and that I was sure he would subscribe immediately. Whereupon Joyce laughed. "He'll never subscribe," said he.

Still, I thought he would.

"Will you bet on it?" Joyce asked. I took him up. It was to be a box of Voltigeurs, the little cigars he liked, against a silk handkerchief (to dry my eyes on?).

Presently I received the following letter from Shaw—which he gave me his permission to print.

Dear Madam,

I have read fragments of *Ulysses* in its serial form. It is a revolting record of a disgusting phase of civilization, but it is a truthful one; and I should like to put a cordon round Dublin; round up every male person in it between the ages of 15 and 30; force them to read all that foul mouthed, foul minded derision and obscenity. To you possibly it may appeal as art; you are probably (you see I don't know you) a young barbarian beglamoured by the excitements and enthusiasms that art stirs up in passionate material; but to me it is all hideously real: I have walked those streets and know those shops and have heard and taken part in those conversations. I escaped from them to England at the age of twenty; and forty years later have learnt from the books of Mr. Joyce that Dublin is still what it was, and young men are still drivelling in slack-jawed blackguardism just as they were in 1870. It is, however, some consolation to find that at last somebody has felt deeply enough about it to face the horror of writing it all down and using his literary genius to force people to face it. In Ireland they try to make a cat cleanly by rubbing its nose in its own filth. Mr. Joyce has tried the same treatment on the human subject. I hope it may prove successful.

I am aware that there are other qualities and other passages in *Ulysses*; but they do not call for any special comment from me.

I must add, as the prospectus implies an invitation to purchase, that I am an elderly Irish gentleman, and if you imagine that any Irishman, much less an elderly one, would pay 150 francs for such a book, you little know my countrymen.

Faithfully,
G. Bernard Shaw

So Joyce was right. And he won his box of Voltigeurs.

I thought the letter from Shaw quite characteristic and very entertaining. His description of me as a "young barbarian beglamoured by the excitements and enthusiasms that art stirs up in passionate material" made me laugh. It seemed to me that he had taken a great deal of trouble to express what he felt about *Ulysses,* and as for his purchasing it, he wasn't obliged to do that. But I must confess I was disappointed.

I let the thing drop, because I was very busy. Ezra Pound, so I heard from Joyce, did take it up, however. I didn't see any of the letters that passed between Pound and Shaw, but evidently, judging by a post card Joyce showed me, Shaw had the last word. It was a card with a reproduction from a painting of Christ's entombment, with the four Marys in tears around Him. Underneath this picture, Shaw had written: "J. J. being put into his tomb by his editresses after the refusal of G.B.S. to subscribe to *Ulysses.*" Then the question: "Do I have to like everything you like, Ezra? As for me, I take care of the pence and let the Pounds take care of themselves."

Joyce was much amused by Shaw's card.

In spite of Shaw, other "elderly Irishmen" did pay 150 francs for *Ulysses.* Some of them even went in for the Dutch paper signed copies at 350 francs.

SEVEN

Valery Larbaud

Joyce said one day that he would like to meet some of the French writers. Shakespeare and Company was very proud of being the godchild of Valery Larbaud, one of the most admired writers in France, and I decided that Joyce and Larbaud should certainly know each other.

Larbaud's novel *Barnabooth*, more or less autobiographical, so fascinated the younger generation that they hesitated whether to be his Barnabooth or Gide's Lafcadio. His other works were also great favorites with the younger generation. His first novel, with its Spanish title, *Fermina Márquez*, was about his school days. He was sent to a school attended by a great many Argentinians, and it was there that he learned to speak Spanish like a native. The volume of short stories called *Enfantines* is perhaps the most concentrated Larbaud of all. "*Larbaldiens*" or, in English, "Larbaldians," was the name by which his many fans were known.

Larbaud was a delightful essayist as well. His writing was the kind that Cyril Connolly said (I forget the exact words) one rolled over one's tongue.

It's a pity that Larbaud is so little known in the United States. In South America he is a favorite; my compatriots, with a few exceptions, are only beginning to find out that there is a

Larbaud. Mr. Justin O'Brien was an early Larbaldian; Eugene Jolas, being bilingual, also appreciated Larbaud's delicate flavor. I am told that William Jay Smith has translated and published his *poèmes par un riche amateur* (meaning Barnabooth) under the title *Poems of a Multimillionaire*. Perhaps more of my countrymen will now be able to enjoy his work. His "bouquet," which reminds me of certain French wines, must be difficult to render in translation. And that may be one of the reasons why a writer with Larbaud's reputation in France is not better known in America.

The name Larbaud is associated with a spring—one of Vichy's famous springs, the Larbaud-St. Yorre, which was discovered by Larbaud's father. The family fortune was derived from it. His mother was descended from an old Bourbonnais family, of Swiss origin, so Larbaud told me, and Protestant.

Valery was a small child when his father died, and was brought up by his mother and an aunt, neither of whom understood him. Why, they complained, did he spend his time reading and, as soon as he could hold a pencil, writing, instead of playing outdoors like other little boys? Luckily for French letters, Valery Larbaud went on writing.

What brought Larbaud and me together was his love of American literature. It was my job to introduce to him our new writers, and every time he left the bookshop, he carried away another armful of their books. He met there, too, live specimens of the new generation.

One day Larbaud brought me a present, or, rather, a present for his godchild Shakespeare and Company. He drew out of its tissue-paper wrappings a little china Shakespeare's House, a childhood possession of his. But this was not all. From a box bearing the name of a well-known firm of toy-soldier makers, Lefèvre, came George Washington and his staff, mounted on prancing horses of different colors; and a company of West Point cadets. This detachment of our forces, as Larbaud explained, was to guard the House of Shakespeare.

Larbaud had superintended the making of these toy soldiers,

which, since he had consulted documents at the Bibliothèque Nationale, were accurate in every detail, down to their buttons. He himself had painted each of these by hand. He said he couldn't trust anybody else with the buttons.

I always kept our armed forces in a small cabinet near the door as you entered the shop. Its glass window was fastened by a secret spring to guard these irresistible little men from rape by my children and animal customers.

Larbaud, curiously enough for such a peace lover, possessed an enormous army, and a growing one, of toy soldiers. He complained bitterly that they were beginning to crowd him out of his rooms, but he made no effort to control them. He and his friend and competitor, Pierre de Lanux, were always on the lookout for rare pieces, and they would go to the ends of the earth to pick up an item they lacked. They traded with each other and with fellow collectors, planned campaigns, and sometimes invited privileged friends to review the troops. Adrienne and I had the honor to be present on one of these occasions, and when we saw the housing conditions at his place, we didn't wonder that Larbaud was uneasy. Troops had invaded his little flat; soldiers were swarming all over the place. Yet he assured us that a large percentage of them were in boxes under the bed.

The soldiers perhaps accounted for another hobby of Larbaud's—his colors. They were blue, yellow, and white, and so were even his cufflinks and his ties. He had his colors flying from the roof of his country house whenever he was in it, which wasn't often, since he preferred to be in Paris or traveling about. Larbaud-Barnabooth was a great traveler and also a great linguist. He knew English so well that he could get into a discussion over Shakespeare's use of the word "motley" with Shakespeare scholars in the *Times Literary Supplement.*

Personally, Larbaud was charming. His large eyes were beautiful and had the kindest expression in them. He was of heavy build; his head was set close to the shoulders. His hands were one of his chief beauties, and he was proud of them. Also, he was proud of his feet, which he crowded into shoes a size smaller than was comfortable. One of his charms was his way of laughing—shaking soundlessly, and blushing. And in quoting a line from some poem he liked, he would turn pale.

But it is to Adrienne's collected essays, *Les Gazettes d'Adrienne Monnier*, that one must go for the best description of Larbaud.

Larbaud, when he visited the bookshop, always asked me what he should read in English, and one time when he came I asked him if he had seen any of the writings of the Irishman James Joyce. He said that he had not, so I gave him *A Portrait of the Artist as a Young Man*. He brought it back soon, saying that it interested him very much, and that he would like to meet the author.

I arranged a meeting between the two writers at Shakespeare and Company on Christmas Eve, 1920. They immediately became great friends. Perhaps I realize more than anyone what the friendship of Valery Larbaud meant to Joyce. Such generosity and unselfishness toward a fellow writer as Larbaud showed to Joyce is indeed rare.

Larbaud had yet to make the acquaintance of *Ulysses*. Hearing that he was laid up with the grippe, I thought this was the right moment for Mr. Bloom to introduce himself. I bundled up all the numbers of the *Little Review* containing parts of *Ulysses*, and sent them to the invalid with some flowers.

The very next day I had a letter from Larbaud in which he said that he was "raving mad over *Ulysses*," and that since he had read Whitman, "when I was eighteen," he had not been so enthusiastic about any book. "It is wonderful! As great as Rabelais!"

Larbaud followed his praise of *Ulysses* by plans to boost Joyce's work. As soon as he was able to leave his bed, he hurried around to the Maison des Amis des Livres to draw up his plans with Adrienne. In a letter to me, he had said he intended to translate and publish in a review some passages from

Ulysses. He also announced that he was going to do an article on Joyce for the *Nouvelle Revue Française*, and he accepted Adrienne's suggestion that he begin by giving a talk on the subject at her bookshop. To illustrate it, he would read his translations. Then they agreed that something from the English text should be read as well. Adrienne and Larbaud agreed that the Joyce reading, or "séance," should be on a paying basis for Joyce's benefit.

Joyce was asked to choose the extract from *Ulysses* to be read in English, and he chose one from the Sirens. We got hold of the gifted young actor Jimmy Light, one of the *Little Review* crowd then in Montparnasse. He consented to recite the piece on condition that Joyce coach him in it; so now their two voices were heard in the back room of my bookshop, repeating the words: "Bald Pat was a waiter hard of hearing. . . ."

Ulysses, meanwhile, was being set into type. The printers, like everyone else connected with this great work, had long since found out that it was invading their lives, and not only were they resigned, but they entered more and more into the spirit of it. They followed my orders to supply Joyce with all the proofs he wanted, and he was insatiable. Every proof was covered with additional text, as Joyce lovers may see at the Yale University Library, which has in its keeping the set of corrected proofs of *Ulysses* that belong to my friend Marian Willard Johnson. They are all adorned with the Joycean rockets and myriads of stars guiding the printers to words and phrases all around the margins. Joyce told me that he had written a third of *Ulysses* on the proofs.

Up to the last minute, the long-suffering printers in Dijon were getting back these proofs, with new things to be inserted somehow, whole paragraphs, even, dislocating pages.

M. Darantiere warned me that I was going to have a lot of extra expense with these proofs. He suggested that I call Joyce's attention to the danger of going beyond my depth; perhaps his appetite for proofs might be curbed. But no, I wouldn't hear

R , Muhammad, the Bride of Lammermoor, Peter the Hermit, Peter the Packer, Dark Rosaleen, Patrick / Shakespeare,

So anyhow Terry brought the three pints Joe was standing and begob the sight nearly left my eyes when I saw him land out a quid. O, as true as I'm telling you. A goodlooking sovereign.

— And there's more where that came from, says he.

— Were you robbing the poorbox, Joe? say I?

— Sweat of my brow, says Joe. 'Twas the prudent member gave me the wheeze.

— I saw him before I met you, says I, sloping around by Pill lane and Greek street with his cod's eye counting up all the guts of the fish.

Who comes through Michan's land, bedight in sable armour? O'Bloom, the son of Rory: it is he. Impervious to fear is Rory's son: he of the prudent soul.

— For the old woman of Prince's street, says the citizen, the subsidised organ. The pledgebound party on the floor of the house. And look at this blasted rag, says he. Look at this, says he. *The Irish Independent*, if you please, founded by Parnell to be the workingman's friend. Listen to the births and deaths in the *Irish all for Ireland Independent* and I'll thank you and the marriages.

And he starts reading them out:

— Gordon, Barnfield Crescent, Exeter; Redmayne of Iffley, Saint Anne's on Sea, the wife of William T. Redmayne, of a son. How's that, eh? Wright and Flint, Vincent and Gillett to Rotha Marion daughter of Rosa and the late George Alfred Gillett 179 Clapham Road, Stockwell, Playwood and Ridsdale at Saint Jude's Kensington by the very reverend Dr Forrest, Dean of Worcester, eh? Deaths. Bristow, at Whitehall lane, London: Carr, Stoke Newington of gastritis and heart disease: Cockburn, at the Moat house, Chepstow...

— I know that fellow, says Joe, from bitter experience.

— Cockburn. Dimsey, wife of David Dimsey, late of the admiralty: Miller, Tottenham, aged eightyfive: Welsh, June 12, at 35 Canning Street, Liverpool, Isabella Helen. How's that for a national press, eh? How's that for Martin Murphy, the Bantry robber?

— Ah, well, says Joe, handing round the boose. Thanks be to God they had the start of us. Drink that, citizen.

— I will, says he, honourable person.

— Health, Joe, says I. And all down the form.

Ah! Ow! Don't be talking! I was blue mouldy for the want of that pint. Declare to God I could hear it hit the pit of my stomach with a click.

And lo, as they quaffed their cup of joy, a godlike messenger came

Page of proof of the first edition of ULYSSES with changes by the author of such a thing. *Ulysses* was to be as Joyce wished, in every respect.

I wouldn't advise "real" publishers to follow my example, nor authors to follow Joyce's. It would be the death of publishing. My case was different. It seemed natural to me that the efforts and sacrifices on my part should be proportionate to the greatness of the work I was publishing.

12 Rue de l'Odéon

In the midst of all this, Shakespeare and Company moved around the corner to the rue de l'Odéon. The new premises, like the old, were a discovery of Adrienne's. She noticed that the antique dealer at No. 12 was looking for someone to take over her lease, and came rushing to let me know. I hurried to No. 12. What luck to find a place in the rue de l'Odéon, and opposite Adrienne's, too. I had hardly dared hope for that. The new shop was larger than the old, and there were two tiny rooms above that went with it.

So, in the summer of 1921, Myrsine and I were busy moving Shakespeare and Company over to the rue de l'Odéon: all the books, the baskets of unanswered correspondence marked "Urgent," the *Ulysses* and other Joycean business, the various publications that I was distributing, the little reviews, the Man Ray portraits of our contemporaries, the Whitman manuscripts, and the Blake drawings.

When we began sorting things out in the new shop, Aunt Agnes's Walt Whitman manuscripts were missing, and that dampened my spirits. I had almost abandoned hope of finding them among all these scattered oddments when my sister Holly, who was present at the moving, asked me if I was sure I had looked everywhere. Sisters can be very annoying. Of course I had. But Holly said, "With my method you always find things." "What's your method?" I asked, not much interested. "Well," said Holly, "you look at every single thing everywhere and what you're looking for is bound to turn up." "Is that so?" said I, and paid no more attention to her. I saw her poking around, with this method of hers; a sheer waste of time. Then she held up some papers and asked, "Is it these?" And it was. I was so glad. It would have been a bad start in the shop at No. 12 if Walt had deserted us.

So Shakespeare and Company in 1921 moved to the rue de l'Odéon and Americanized it; and very very French though Adrienne was, we did our best to annex her, too.

The cafés at Saint Germain des Prés in pre-Sarte-Beauvoir days were patronized by quiet literary people, though you might see Ezra Pound at the Deux Magots or Léon-Paul Fargue across the street at Lipp's. Except for our two bookshops, where things were always happening, our rue de l'Odéon, a few steps down from the Boulevard Saint Germain, was as restful as a little street in a provincial town. The only time there was any traffic was when the audiences on their way to or from the Odéon Theatre at the upper end of the street streamed past. The performances, like the street, were rather provincial, though occasionally one of the great producers took over the theatre for a while. Antoine, I remember, put on *King Lear*, and even Copeau moved in at one time—his scenery was so austere that Léon-Paul Fargue called the show "The Calvin Follies." The Théâtre de l'Odéon fulfilled Adrienne's dream of living in a street "with a public building at one end."

Soon after I decided to bring out *Ulysses*, John Quinn, the possessor of the manuscript, came to inspect conditions at Shakespeare and Company. He was a good-looking man, and he interested me. I admired his taste. He had collected manuscripts by Yeats and Conrad as well as by Joyce, and the drawings of Wyndham Lewis; and there was his fine collection of Impressionists—which brought such a high price later in Paris. But I found him rather testy and explosive. Our little premises in the rue Dupuytren, where he found us doing business on this first visit, didn't make a good impression on him, I fear. There was a deplorable lack of office furniture and fittings, and this, coupled with the fact that I was a woman, aroused his suspicions. I could see that he was going to keep a stern eye on me in this *Ulysses* affair, and I was made to feel that I was very much to blame for being "another woman," as he called me.

Joyce and I were fond of the little shop in the rue Dupuytren, and quite missed it, but it was just as well that we had moved to larger quarters and a wider street by the time John Quinn paid his second and, as it turned out, his last, visit. There was more room for Quinn to walk up and down as he lectured me on my responsibilities or grumbled away over all those works of art Pound had lured him into buying, particularly "that stuff of Wyndham Lewis" and "this rubbish of Yeats— a ragpicker wouldn't look at it." He remarked that he was glad *Ulysses* "wasn't going to come out in that shanty," meaning the shop in the rue Dupuytren.

Poor Quinn! He was so burly, and had such a good heart! I'm glad that I had this brief contact with him and that I listened patiently to his complaints—from what I heard later he must already have been a very sick man.

Greek Blue and Circe

The months passed. Far-off subscribers were beginning to get restless; "the autumn of 1921" came and went, and *Ulysses* wasn't even in their Christmas stocking. Shakespeare and Company was in danger of being had up for swindling the public. The subscribers couldn't ask for their money back, since they hadn't paid anything yet, but I got peremptory letters. I had one from T. E. Lawrence, I remember, demanding his copy of *Ulysses*. I had no time, unfortunately, to explain to him that I, too, was fighting a battle, though not in the desert.

Subscribers in Paris, thanks to the almost daily bulletins in the press, were kept in touch with developments. My newspaper friends looked on *Ulysses*, and rightly, as an event of world-wide importance, almost a sporting event, and there was actually an article about *Ulysses* in the British sheet the *Sporting Times*, known as the Pink 'Un—but that was after the book appeared.

One of my problems was the paper for the binding of *Ulysses*. Joyce's natural desire to have his book dressed in the Greek blue was the cause of one of our worst difficulties. Who would have dreamed that the lovely blue of the Greek flag was not to be found? Again and again, Darantiere came up to Paris, and we matched blues, only to discover that the new sample didn't go with the Greek flag, which was kept flying at Shakespeare and Company in honor of Odysseus. Alas! merely to look at that flag gave me a headache.

Darantiere's search took him to Germany, where it ended with the discovery of the right blue—but this time it was the wrong paper. He solved this problem by getting the color lithographed on white cardboard, which explains why the insides of the covers were white.

In the delightful old vine-covered printing house of Darantiere, in Dijon, speed was accelerated and the lights were on all night. Dijon, in the Côte d'Or, a region of famous wines, of art treasures, fine cooking, those candied black currants in liqueur, and, of course, the specialty of Dijon, mustard, to which was now added that "hot" book *Ulysses*. M. Darantiere, who was so fond of cooking special dishes and tasting the fine wines that went along with them, no longer had time to linger at table with the young printer friend who kept house with him, nor to look at his collection of old pottery or his valuable library. *Ulysses* had taken over Darantiere.

Presently M. Darantiere informed me that the printing had caught up with the supply of text. It was the Circe episode that was holding us back; Circe was balking.

Joyce had been trying in vain for some time to get this episode typed. Nine typists had failed in the attempt. The eighth, Joyce told me, threatened in her despair to throw herself out of the window. As for the ninth, she rang the bell at his door and, when it was opened, threw the pages she had done on the floor, then rushed away down the street and disappeared forever. "If she had given me her name and address, at least I could have paid her for her work," Joyce said. He hadn't caught her name when a friend introduced him.

After that, he had given up trying to get the Circe typed. With sighs, he brought his "piece" and left it in my hands. I told him not to worry, I would look for volunteers to go on with it.

The first to volunteer her services in the cause of Circe was my sister Cyprian. She had to be at the film studio all day, but she always woke up at four o'clock in the morning, and she offered to put in some early hours on Circe.

Cyprian was an admirer of *Ulysses,* and an expert reader of undecipherable handwriting because her own was that kind. Deciphering the Joycean signs, word by word, she was slowly progressing with the work when suddenly her film took her off to other scenes, and I had to find another volunteer.

Cyprian's place was taken by my friend Raymonde Linossier. As soon as she heard of the fix I was in, she offered to do the copying of the Circe; it would help to pass the time when she was on night duty at her sick father's bedside.

She took over the job and, considering that English was not her native language, was making wonderful progress when she, too, had to give it up. Immediately, however, she found someone to replace her, and Volunteer No. 3, an English friend of Raymonde's, now very kindly agreed to go on with it. The husband of this lady, from what Raymonde told me, held some post at the British Embassy.

I had hardly time to rejoice over this good luck when Raymonde came in great consternation to announce a disaster. Her friend's husband had happened to pick up the manuscript she was copying, and, after one glance at it, had thrown it into the fire.

I broke the news to Joyce. The only thing to do, he said,

was to ask John Quinn in New York for the loan of his manuscript of the missing pages as soon as it reached him—it was
then in mid-ocean on its way to him.

I cabled Quinn, and wrote to him, but he flatly refused to
release his manuscript, even to Joyce himself, who also sent
him a cable and a letter. I asked my mother, who was in
Princeton, to tackle Quinn. She spoke to him on the telephone;
he flew into a rage, and used language unfit for a lady like my
mother. It was plain that Quinn meant to hold on to his manuscript.

I asked him if he would be willing to let someone copy the
pages I needed. He wouldn't permit that either. At last, however, he compromised by having them photographed. In due
time, I received the reproductions, and because these were
pages of Joyce's "fair copy," instead of the illegible manuscript we had been struggling with, they were soon copied
and whisked off to Darantiere.

Joyce's handwriting, which had once been quite legible, was
getting, with its ellipses and barely perceptible signs, to be as
difficult to read as ogham. His increasing eye trouble during the
Circe period accounted, I think, for the undecipherable handwriting in certain parts of that episode.

Ulysses, like everything else of Joyce's, was written entirely
by hand. He used blunt black pencils—he found the ones he
wanted at Smith's in Paris—and pencils of different colors to
distinguish the parts he was working on. Fountain pens he
didn't understand at all. They bewildered him. Once I found
him struggling to fill one, covering himself with ink as he did
so. Years later, he did think of using a typewriter, and asked
me to get him a Remington Noiseless. He soon swapped it for
Adrienne's noisy one, and, so far as I know, never used either
of them.

EIGHT

Joyce's Eyes

I hoped, now that our Circe troubles were over, that things would go smoothly—or at least more smoothly. On the contrary, we had a disaster far greater than any other that had befallen us. Joyce had strained his eyes, and he now came down with an acute attack of iritis.

His children came running to fetch me one day: "Babbo," as they called their father, wanted to see me at once. Hurrying to the little hotel in the rue de l'Université, where they were living at the time, I found Joyce lying very ill. He was suffering terribly. Mrs. Joyce was tending him. With a bucket of ice water beside her, she was constantly renewing the compresses on his eyes. She had kept this up for hours, and looked worn out. "When the pain is unbearable he gets up and walks the floor," she said.

I saw immediately that, dreadful though the pain in his eyes was, he was thinking of something else and was extremely agitated about it. He told me what was upsetting him. A famous specialist whom a friend had brought to see him had just left, saying he would have to operate at once, and was sending an ambulance to take Joyce to his clinic. That was why I had been sent for in such haste. He was determined to prevent another operation like the one in Zurich, performed at the height of an attack. He was not going to allow this mistake to be made again. I was to get hold of my oculist—he had heard me speak of him—and bring him to the hotel before the other doctor whisked him off to his clinic.

I scooted over to the rue de la Paix, where, among all those dressmaking establishments, my oculist had his office, and burst in on him. Dr. Louis Borsch, a compatriot of mine, had been very kind when I once consulted him at the little clinic he ran on the Left Bank for students and working people. He listened very kindly now to the account I gave him of Joyce's woeful situation, but though I beseeched him to go to him at once, he said he was sorry, he couldn't go to the bedside of a patient another physician was looking after. Seeing my despair, he said he would see Joyce, but Joyce must come to him. I told him that Joyce was too ill to leave his bed, but Dr. Borsch was firm. "Get him over here as soon as you can," he said.

So I flew back to the hotel. Joyce said, "Let's be off," and Nora and I got the poor man out of his bed, downstairs, and into a taxi. We managed to get him across town and up to the doctor's waiting room, where, almost unconscious with pain, he collapsed into a big armchair.

Oh, the wait in that waiting room, under the gaze of those silver-framed crowned heads with grateful inscriptions that adorned the grand piano.

Joyce's turn finally came and, supported by the nurse, he went in.

He knew it was glaucoma; the diagnosis was no surprise to him. He only wanted to know Dr. Borsch's opinion on the subject of the proper time to operate. The doctor said an operation would be necessary, but though some of his colleagues wouldn't agree with him, he preferred to wait till the acute attack of iritis was over, even if the vision suffered from the delay. An operation when the eye was inflamed might, if it was successful, restore the sight; on the other hand, the sight in that eye might be totally destroyed; and Dr. Borsch said that he was not willing to take that risk.

This was just what Joyce wanted to hear, and he was immensely relieved. He made up his mind at once to put himself in the hands of Dr. Borsch. An operation was to be performed as soon as he had sufficiently recovered from the attack of iritis.

Dr. Borsch was the pupil of a great Viennese specialist, and he himself had a wide reputation. He attended Joyce with the utmost devotion for many years; and his fees amounted to so little that Joyce, showing me one of Dr. Borsch's bills, seemed to feel quite insulted that it was so small. Dr. Borsch did all he could to stop the progress and to deal with the complications of Joyce's terrible disease. His sight, nevertheless, gradually diminished, but it would be unjust to blame it on Dr. Borsch, as perhaps some people did.

Finally, in the hope of saving what little was left of his sight, Joyce went back to Zurich to consult a man who was considered one of the three great authorities in Europe, Dr. Alfred Vogt. Joyce had heard a great deal about this doctor, and told me about an instrument he had invented. These instruments were specially made in Berlin, one at a time. Each was adapted to the particular operation to be made, and was never used more than once. Each one cost him a hundred dollars; and if Dr. Vogt discovered the slightest flaw in one, he threw it away.

Joyce told me in detail how Dr. Vogt proceeded with a case. He first made a map of the eye to be operated on, and studied it until he knew its "geography" by heart. When, as in Joyce's case, the eye was covered by a sort of opaque curtain, the instrument penetrated it in such a way as to pierce an opening, through which, to a certain extent, the patient could see.

When Joyce came to see me after this operation in Zurich, I noticed that he could distinguish outlines of objects, didn't bump into things when he moved about, and, with his glasses and the help of two magnifying glasses, could read very large type. Alas, however, for Mr. Earwicker. Joyce, always abnormally sensitive to sound, must henceforth depend almost entirely on his ears.

At Larbaud's

When Joyce was recovering from the attack of iritis, and before his operation, Larbaud, who was going to be away from Paris for a month, decided that a hotel wasn't a comfortable place for an invalid and invited the Joyces to move into his apartment, a very kind thought of Larbaud's, and surprising when one knew his then rather fastidious bachelor's ways. (He got married later.)

He lived at No. 71 in the old rue du Cardinal Lemoine, one of those streets behind the Pantheon that run down the Montagne Ste. Geneviève toward the Seine. You went through a big gateway, and down a long passage opening into a kind of English-looking square with shady trees around it. Larbaud's apartment was in one of the houses behind these trees. It was a secluded spot and one where Larbaud liked to retire for long periods of solitude and work, for what he would warn all his friends was to be a *"clôture"*—a retreat. No one was admitted at such times except his charwoman.

So now, in these neat little rooms of Larbaud's, with the polished floors, the antique furniture, the toy soldiers, and the valuable books in their fine bindings, the Joyces were installed.

On Larbaud's bed lay Joyce, his eyes bandaged and a smile on his lips as he listened to the conversation in the next room between his daughter and the charwoman. All household communications were through Lucia, whose French was the most fluent—and, as usual with people who came in contact with Joyce, the charwoman was extremely interested in him.

"She always refers to me as 'he,' " Joyce said. " 'How is he now? What is he doing? What does he say? Is he going to get up? Is he ever hungry? Does he suffer?' " All in low tones but quite perceptible to Joyce's sensitive hearing.

Sometimes you would find Bob McAlmon sitting at Joyce's bedside, amusing him with the latest gossip about "the Crowd" and particularly with his American language and his nasal drawl. McAlmon was often with Joyce and his family in those days. Paul-Emile Bécat, Adrienne's brother-in-law, did a drawing of Joyce and McAlmon together.

Garlic in a Sponge

The Left Bank clinic where Joyce had his operation was a small two-storied building on a corner where two streets met. The names of these streets, as Joyce observed, were quite appropriate: rue du Cherche-Midi ("Southern-Seeking Street," would you translate it?) and rue du Regard.

The street door opened into the waiting room downstairs, where the patients, seated on long wooden benches, waited, often a long time, for the doctor to drop in on his way home after morning rounds. He was overworked, poor Dr. Borsch, and I wonder when he ever managed to snatch a meal. When he did, it must have been a big one, for he was as fat as Santa Claus. At the back of the waiting room was the office, about the size of a coat closet, barely large enough to hold the doctor, his nurse—who was also rather stout—and an ordinary-sized patient.

Upstairs were two little bedrooms for in-patients. Joyce occupied one of these. He wouldn't stay anywhere without Nora, so she occupied the other. She complained, with reason, of the lack of modern comfort; it was certainly a quaint establishment. Joyce, on the contrary, found the place interesting. He liked the doctor, and did a take-off of his "Yankee drawl" for me, and of his mumbled words as he bent over him: "Too bad ye got that kickup in your eye." Joyce also liked his nurse, the stout lady, who ran the establishment and the patients, cooked the meals, and assisted the doctor. "She grows garlic in a sponge on the window," he told me, "to season our dishes with." She was crusty at times with other patients, but with Monsieur "Juass" never. He was her pet patient. And no wonder! He was, I'm sure, the most uncomplaining sufferer and the most considerate sick person she had ever known.

An eye operation must be a dreadful ordeal, particularly for someone as sensitive as Joyce. Conscious, he watched it going on, and, as he told me, the instrument looming up in front of his eye appeared like a great ax.

When he was recovering from his operation, he lay with bandaged eyes, hour after hour, never in the least impatient. He had no time to be bored; so many ideas came into his head.

Indeed, how could anyone as inexhaustibly creative as Joyce be bored? Besides, there were his memory exercises. He had kept them up since his early youth, and this accounted for a memory that retained everything he had ever heard. Everything stuck in it, he said.

"Will you please bring 'The Lady of the Lake,'" he asked me one day. The next time I went to see him, I had the "Lady" with me. "Open it," he said, "and read me a line." I did so, from a page chosen at random. After the first line, I stopped, and he recited the whole page and the next without a single mistake. I'm convinced that he knew by heart, not only "The Lady of the Lake," but a whole library of poetry and prose. He probably read everything before he was twenty, and thenceforth he could find what he needed without taking the trouble of opening a book.

My visits to the clinic were frequent. I took him his mail and read it to him, and also the proofs of *Ulysses*. Letters, I could answer, and, in fact, had been answering for some time. The proofs had to wait. He alone could handle them, because he always wanted to add to the text. I gave him the news from the printers, brought messages from his friends, and told him what was going on at Shakespeare and Company, which he always liked to hear.

I arrived at the clinic one day at the moment when the leeches prescribed by the doctor were being applied. Once they could be persuaded to stick around the eye—not so easy —they drew away the blood and relieved the congestion. The regular nurse was out, and a younger one was replacing her. She and Mrs. Joyce were trying to prevent these wriggling creatures from flopping on the floor instead of waiting their turn around the patient's eye. Uncomplaining, Joyce submitted to this unpleasant ordeal. The leeches reminded me of those that used to stick to our legs in the Russells' swimming pool in Princeton.

Joyce and George Moore

Joyce, as a rule, didn't avoid people. The first time he went out after his operation, however, and turned up at the book-shop, he said he didn't feel that he could meet anyone. I quite understood, and when a tall man with a large face and pink cheeks gazed at the books in the window, then stepped into the shop, I left Joyce to speak to my customer.

The customer introduced himself as George Moore. Our mutual friend Nancy Cunard had promised to bring him to see me, but he couldn't wait for her because he was returning to London the next day. I saw him glancing from time to time at the man standing at the back of the shop, but I kept my promise and didn't introduce him. Finally, the visitor withdrew, rather reluctantly, after a last glance in Joyce's direction.

"Who was that?" Joyce asked. I told him, and he exclaimed: "I'd like to have thanked him for his kindness in obtaining the King's Purse for me." It was the first time he had mentioned this to me—the £100 he had received from the Privy Purse several years before.

On his return to London, George Moore wrote me a charming letter, inviting me to lunch with him in Ebury Street (one of those famous invitations to lunch in Ebury Street) next time I visited London. And he wondered if the man with the black patch over one eye whom he had noticed in the back of my bookshop was James Joyce; he would have liked to meet him.

So I saw my mistake in keeping my promise to Joyce. They

did finally meet in London, however, for the second time, I subsequently learned, though Joyce didn't mention it.

I would have liked to see more of Moore myself. He was exceedingly friendly. He didn't hold the incident in the bookshop against me; on the contrary, he sent me the corrected proofs of his forthcoming play *The Apostle*. I was very fond of George Moore as a writer; and as a person, too, from what I had heard of him from Nancy Cunard, a great friend of his. He died before I had a chance to go to London and lunch with him in Ebury Street.

The Reading at A. Monnier's

The date set for the Joyce reading at Adrienne's bookshop was December 7, 1921—a little less than two months before *Ulysses* appeared.

Larbaud, fearing his translations of extracts from Penelope wouldn't be ready in time, asked Adrienne to look around for someone to help him. Among those who frequented the rue de l'Odéon was a young composer of music, Jacques Benoist-Méchin. He and George Antheil had struck up a friendship after meeting in my bookshop. Young Benoist-Méchin's English was remarkably good, and when Adrienne asked him if he would go to Larbaud's assistance, he accepted gladly, delighted to have an opportunity to work with him on *Ulysses*, on condition, however, that his name be kept out of it, because of his father; the old gentleman, a baron, wouldn't approve of *Ulysses*.

Surprisingly, in the land of Rabelais, *Ulysses* was almost too daring for the France of the twenties. As the time for the Joyce reading approached, Larbaud himself had misgivings, and on the program was the following warning: "*Nous tenons à prevenir le public que certaines des pages qu'on lira sont d'une hardiesse peu commune qui peut très légitimement choquer*" (The audience is warned that certain pages to be read are bolder than is common and might justly offend hearers). Yes, Larbaud, when he arrived at the bookshop, which was so packed that not another person could be squeezed in, was suffering from stage fright. Adrienne had to give him a glass of brandy before he could summon his courage to go in and sit down at the little table, a place that wasn't new to him, since he was one of the favorite readers at Adrienne's "séances." But he actually backed out of an extract or two!

This reading was a triumph for Joyce, and it was a tribute that just at that most critical moment in his career meant much to him. Larbaud's warm praises and his reading of his translated extracts from *Ulysses*, Jimmy Light's successful rendering of the Sirens—all were loudly applauded by the listeners. Louder still was the cheering when Larbaud, after looking everywhere for Joyce, discovered him behind a screen in the back room, dragged him out blushing, and kissed him French fashion on both cheeks.

Adrienne was happy over the success of her plan. I, too, was happy, and thought the French hospitality to the Irish writer James Joyce very touching.

"Saint Harriet"

About that time, the author of *Ulysses* was having a dreadful struggle to make ends meet. I wasn't exactly well to do myself; the Shakespeare and Company shoestring sometimes threatened to give way, and my kind sister Holly's checks and those of my dear Cousin Mary Morris and her granddaughter Marguerite MacCoy in Overbrook, Pennsylvania, were never turned down. Rents in Paris were small, and there were only myself and Myrsine, so, as far as overhead expenses went, there was nothing to worry about. But the books, ah! they were expensive, and when the time came to pay for them, in English and American currency, it usually looked as if Shakespeare and Company was heading for the rocks—and not the ones Mae West talked about.

Now James Joyce was a man who had always supported himself and his family by teaching. At the moment, he was working seventeen hours a day to finish *Ulysses*, but he was earning nothing. Everything in the way of savings or gifts had been swallowed up long ago. My job of publishing *Ulysses* included preventing the author from going under meanwhile. The help that his little bookseller-publisher could give to a family of four persons was, as one may imagine, quite inadequate, but as a rule there was no one else to whom Joyce could turn.

Joyce was extremely scrupulous in money matters. For proof of it, one has only to look at his notebook of student days at the Hôtel Corneille, in which the young medical student jotted down the dates and amounts of borrowed sums and the names of the lenders. The notes also show that the loans were refunded, often the next day, even if it meant starving himself—see the photograph taken in those Paris days. But on the following day, he notes that he has borrowed again the same amount from the same friend. Very amusing, if it weren't so heartbreaking!

Joyce showed me his notebook, smiling rather sheepishly as he did so. It was the same system, but another friend now. Little sums went to and fro between the Shakespearean cashbox and Joyce's pocket. Scraps informing me that "J.J.'s coffers" are empty again still turn up among my papers. The sums were usually small; the borrower's efforts to adapt his demands to the resources of the lender were pathetic.

This went on for a while, and as long as it was on a basis of "*va-et-vient*" it worked. Then, as Joyce's expenses increased, I noticed with alarm that our routine was changing, and that the sums were going to but not fro. In fact, they were taking the form of advances on *Ulysses*. And what could be more natural in ordinary cases? Great as was my admiration for

Ulysses, human beings were more to me than works of art. But my role was that of a publisher, and I had to bring out this book *Ulysses*, and to run a bookshop, and it looked to me as if we might all be going bankrupt pretty soon.

One day, at the verge of disaster, Joyce appeared and, much excited over his news, announced that he had just heard from Miss Harriet Weaver, who was sending him a great deal of money, a sum, he said, that would provide him with an income for the rest of his life!

We both rejoiced over this miracle, he, because Miss Weaver's generosity had removed one of his worst problems, and I, for his sake, but also for my own. It was a tremendous relief to feel that I could now go ahead and publish *Ulysses*, and also that Shakespeare and Company was free of encumbrance, so to speak.

Miss Weaver—"Saint Harriet," Mrs. Jolas told me, was Lucia's name for her—had given Joyce enough for someone else to live on the rest of his life, but not Joyce. It wasn't long before he was again hard up, and Miss Weaver came again to his help. However, we had a moment of relief.

NINE

My Best Customer

A customer we liked, one who gave us no trouble, was that young man you saw almost every morning over there in a corner at Shakespeare and Company, reading the magazines or Captain Marryat or some other book. This was Ernest Hemingway, who turned up in Paris, as I remember, late in 1921. My "best customer," he called himself, a title that no one disputed with him. Great was our esteem for a customer who was not only a regular visitor, but spent money on books, a trait very pleasing to the proprietor of a small book business.

However, he would have endeared himself to me just as much if he hadn't spent a penny in my establishment. I felt the warmest friendship for Ernest Hemingway from the day we met.

Sherwood Anderson, in Chicago, had given his "young friends Mr. and Mrs. Ernest Hemingway" a letter of introduction to me. I have it still, and it reads as follows:

I am writing this note to make you acquainted with my friend Ernest Hemingway, who with Mrs. Hemingway is going to Paris to live, and will ask him to drop it in the mails when he arrives there.

Mr. Hemingway is an American writer instinctively in touch with everything worth while going on here and I know you will find both Mr. and Mrs. Hemingway delightful people to know. . . .

77

But the Hemingways and I had known each other for some time before they remembered to produce Anderson's letter. Hemingway just walked in one day.

I looked up and saw a tall, dark young fellow with a small mustache, and heard him say, in a deep, deep voice, that he was Ernest Hemingway. I invited him to sit down, and, drawing him out, I learned that he was from Chicago originally. I also learned that he had spent two years in a military hospital, getting back the use of his leg. What had happened to his leg? Well, he told me apologetically, like a boy confessing he had been in a scrap, he had got wounded in the knee, fighting in Italy. Would I care to see it? Of course I would. So business at Shakespeare and Company was suspended while he removed his shoe and sock, and showed me the dreadful scars covering his leg and foot. The knee was the worst hurt, but the foot seemed to have been badly injured, too, from a burst of shrapnel, he said. In the hospital, they had thought he was done for; there was even some question of administering the last sacraments. But this was changed, with his feeble consent, to baptism—"just in case they were right."

So Hemingway was baptized. Baptized or not—and I am going to say this whether Hemingway shoots me or not—I have always felt that he was a deeply religious man. Hemingway was a great pal of Joyce's, and Joyce remarked to me one day that he thought it was a mistake, Hemingway's thinking himself such a tough fellow and McAlmon trying to pass himself off as the sensitive type. It was the other way round, he thought. So Joyce found you out, Hemingway!

Hemingway confided to me that before he was out of high school, when he was still "a boy in short pants," his father had died suddenly and in tragic circumstances, leaving him a gun as a sole legacy. He found himself the head of a family, his mother and brothers and sister dependent on him. He had to leave school and begin making a living. He earned his first money in a boxing match, but, from what I gathered, didn't linger in this career. He spoke rather bitterly of his boyhood.

He didn't tell me much about his life after he left school. He earned his living at various jobs, including newspaper work, I believe, then went over to Canada and enlisted in the armed forces. He was so young he had to fake his age to be accepted.

Hemingway was a widely educated young man, who knew many countries and several languages; and he had learned it all at first hand, not in universities. He seemed to me to have gone a great deal farther and faster than any of the young writers I knew. In spite of a certain boyishness, he was exceptionally wise and self-reliant. In Paris, Hemingway had a job as sports correspondent for the Toronto *Star*. No doubt he was already trying his hand at writing fiction.

He brought his young wife, Hadley, to see me. She was an attractive, delightfully jolly person. Of course I took them both around to see Adrienne Monnier. Hemingway's knowledge of French was remarkable, and he managed somehow to find time to read all the French publications as well as ours.

Hemingway's job as sports correspondent took him to all the events in that line, and his linguistic attainments included argot. This world of sports was one into which Hemingway's bookshop pals Adrienne and Sylvia had never penetrated, but we were ready to be enlightened, and Hemingway to enlighten us.

Our studies began with boxing. One evening our educators, Hemingway and Hadley, stopped by for us and we all set off by métro to the mountainous region of Ménilmontant, inhabited by workers, sportsmen, and a certain number of toughs. At the Pelleport station we climbed the steep stairs, Hadley, who was expecting Bumby (John Hadley Hemingway), puffing slightly and assisted by her husband. Hemingway led us to the ring, a tiny one that you had to go through a sort of backyard to reach, and we found seats on narrow benches without backs.

The fights and our instruction began. When, in the preliminary matches, the boys swung their arms around and bled so profusely that we were afraid they were going to bleed to death, Hemingway reassured us; it was only slugging and nosebleed, he said. We learned some of the rules of the game. We were informed, too, that those rather bleary characters strolling in and out, hardly seeming to give the fighters a glance, but discussing something now and again among themselves, were managers who dropped in at rings to look for new and promising material.

By the time the big event came on, our professor was too busy watching the punches to be depended on for any more hints, and his pupils had to do without him.

This last fight led to another—in which the spectators participated. Opinion was divided on the referee's decision; everybody got up on the benches and jumped down on each other —a real Western. What with the socking, the kicking, the yelling, and the surging back and forth, I was afraid we would be "Hemmed" in, and that Hadley would be injured in the melee. Calls for "*Le flic! le flic!*" were heard, but evidently not by the cop whose attendance at all French places of amusement, whether it's the Comédie-Française or a boxing ring in Ménilmontant, is obligatory. We heard Hemingway's voice above the din exclaiming with disapproval: "*Et naturellement le flic est dans la pissottiere!*"

Next, Adrienne and I took up cycling under Hemingway's tuition and influence; not that we did any cycling ourselves, but we attended with our professor the "Six-Jours," that six-day merry-go-round at the Vél d'Hiv, easily the most popular event in the Paris season. Fans went and lived there for the duration, watching more and more listlessly the little monkeymen, hunched over on their bikes, slowly circling the ring or suddenly sprinting, night and day, in an atmosphere of smoke and dust and theatrical stars, and amid the blare of loudspeakers. We did our best to follow what the professor was saying to us, but rarely could we distinguish words above the din. Unfortunately, Adrienne and I could spare only one night for this sport, engrossing though we found it. But what wouldn't have been engrossing in Hemingway's company?

A much more exciting event awaited us. I had had the impression for some time that Hemingway was working hard on some stories. He told me one day he had finished one, and asked if Adrienne and I would care to hear it. Eagerly we attended this event, one that concerned us deeply, for she and I were something like those bleary persons hanging around Pelleport Ring on the lookout for talent. Maybe we didn't know much about boxing, but when it came to writing—that was another thing. Imagine our joy over this first bout of Ernest Hemingway's!

So Hemingway read us one of the stories from *In Our Time*. We were impressed by his originality, his very personal style, his skillful workmanship, his tidiness, his storyteller's gift and sense of the dramatic, his power to create—well, I could go on, but as Adrienne summed him up: "Hemingway has the true writer's temperament" ("*le tempérament authentique d'écrivain*").

Of course, today Hemingway is the acknowledged daddy of modern fiction. You can't open a novel or a short story in France, or in England or Germany or Italy or anywhere else, without noticing that Hemingway has passed that way. He has landed in schoolbooks, which is more fun for the children than they have as a rule and very lucky for them!

Though the question who has influenced such and such a writer has never bothered me, and the adult writer doesn't stay awake at night to wonder who has influenced him, I do think Hemingway readers should know who taught him to write: it was Ernest Hemingway. And, like all authentic writers, he knew that to make it "good," as he called it, you had to work.

Adrienne Monnier was Hemingway's first French fan, and she was the first to publish a story of his in French. "The Undefeated" came out in her magazine, *Le Navire d'Argent*, and it attracted a great deal of attention among its readers.

Hemingway's readers were usually won over by a first contact. I remember Jonathan Cape's enthusiasm over his first Hemingway. Mr. Cape, Colonel Lawrence's and Joyce's publisher in England, asked me, on one of his visits to Paris, what American he should publish. "Here, read Hemingway!" I said —and that is how Mr. Cape became Hemingway's English publisher.

Hemingway was serious and competent in whatever he did, even when he went in for the care of an infant. After a brief visit to Canada, Hadley and Hemingway came back bringing another "best customer," John Hadley Hemingway. Dropping in one morning and seeing him giving the baby his bath, I was amazed at his deft handling of Bumby. Hemingway *père* was justly proud, and asked me if I didn't think he had a future as a nursemaid.

Bumby was frequenting Shakespeare and Company before he could walk. Holding his son carefully, though sometimes upside down, Hemingway went on reading the latest periodicals, which required some technique, I must say. As for Bumby, anything was all right as long as he was with his adored Papa. His first steps were to what he called "Sylver Beach's." I can see them, father and son, coming along hand in hand up the street. Bumby, hoisted on a high stool, observed his old man gravely, never showing any impatience, waiting to be lifted from his high perch at last; it must have seemed a long wait sometimes. Then I would watch the two of them as they set off, not for home, since they had to keep out of Hadley's way till the housekeeping was done, but to the bistrot around the corner; there, seated at a table, their drinks before them— Bumby's was a grenadine—they went over all the questions of the day.

Everybody at that time had been in Spain, and varied were the impressions. Gertrude Stein and Alice B. Toklas had found it very amusing. Others had gone to a bullfight, been shocked, and come away before the end. The bullfight had been written up from the moral and the sexual point of view, and as a bright-colored sport, picturesque and all that. The Spanish themselves usually found anything foreigners said about *los toros* bewildering and, besides, technically unsound.

Hemingway, unlike the others, set out to learn and to write about the bulls in his usual serious, competent manner. So we have, in *Death in the Afternoon,* a complete treatise on bull-fighting, one that my Spanish friends, the most difficult to please, have acknowledged as excellent. And some of Hemingway's finest writing is in this book.

Good writers are so rare that if I were a critic, I would only try to point out what I think makes them reliable and enjoyable. For how can anyone explain the mystery of creation?

Hemingway can take any amount of criticism—from himself; he is his own severest critic, but, like all his fellow-writers, he is hypersensitive to the criticism of others. It's true that some critics are terribly expert in sticking the sharp penpoint into the victim and are delighted when he squirms. Wyndham Lewis succeeded in making Joyce squirm. And his article on Hemingway entitled "The Dumb Ox," which the subject of it picked up in my bookshop, I regret to say, roused him to such anger that he punched the heads off three dozen tulips, a birthday gift. As a result, the vase upset its contents over the books, after which Hemingway sat down at my desk and wrote a check payable to Sylvia Beach for a sum that covered the damage twice over.

As a bookseller and librarian, I paid more attention to titles perhaps than others who simply rush past the threshold of a book without ringing the bell. I think Hemingway's titles should be awarded first prize in any contest. Each of them is a poem, and their mysterious power over readers contributes to Hemingway's success. His titles have a life of their own, and they have enriched the American vocabulary.

TEN

First Copies of *Ulysses*

There was a rumor that *Ulysses* might be appearing very soon.
The page proofs all the way to the end of Penelope were now
in my hands.

Joyce's birthday, the second of February, was approaching;
and I knew he had set his heart on celebrating the event of
Ulysses the same day.

I had a conversation with Darantiere. He said the printers
had done their best, but that I must wait a little longer for
Ulysses. It wasn't possible to have it ready by February 2. I
asked him if he would please do what was impossible—have
at least one copy of *Ulysses* to put in Joyce's hands on his
birthday.

He made no promises, but I knew Darantiere, and I was not
surprised when I received a telegram from him on February
1st, asking me to meet the express from Dijon at 7 A.M. the next
day; the conductor would have two copies of *Ulysses* for me.

I was on the platform, my heart going like the locomotive,
as the train from Dijon came slowly to a standstill and I saw
the conductor getting off, holding a parcel and looking around
for someone—me. In a few minutes, I was ringing the door-
bell at the Joyces' and handing them Copy No. 1 of *Ulysses*.
It was February 2, 1922.

Copy No. 2 was for Shakespeare and Company, and I made the mistake of putting it on view in the window. The news spread rapidly in Montparnasse and outlying districts, and next day, before the bookshop was open, subscribers were lining up in front of it, pointing to *Ulysses*. No use explaining that, except for two copies, *Ulysses* wasn't out. They seemed about to snatch my *Ulysses* from the window and would no doubt have done so and divided it into enough pieces to go around if I hadn't acted quickly and removed it to a safer place.

Joyce expressed his appreciation of his birthday present in a note. "I cannot let today pass," he wrote, "without thanking you for all the trouble and worry you have given yourself about my book during the last year." And he celebrated the appearance of *Ulysses* by writing some jocular verses to its publisher. They were as follows:

> Who is Sylvia, what is she
> That all our scribes commend her?
> Yankee, young and brave is she
> The west this pace did lend her
> That all books might published be.
>
> Is she rich as she is brave
> For wealth oft daring misses?
> Throngs about her rant and rave
> To subscribe for *Ulysses*
> But, having signed, they ponder grave.
>
> Then to Sylvia let us sing
> Her daring lies in selling.
> She can sell each mortal thing
> That's boring beyond telling
> To her let us buyers bring.
>
> > J. J.
> > after
> > W. S.

Here at last was *Ulysses*, in a Greek blue jacket, bearing the title and the author's name in white letters. Here were the seven hundred and thirty-two pages "complete as written," and an average of one to half-a-dozen typographical errors per page—the publisher apologized for them on a little slip inserted in the copies.

The period immediately following the publication of his book was so exciting that Joyce couldn't keep away from his publisher for fear of missing something. He applied himself to helping (?) us with the parcels; he had even found out that the copies weighed one kilo, five hundred and fifty grams each. We had noticed this, too, when we started toting the parcels to the post office around the corner. Lavishing glue on the labels, the floor, and his hair, he urged me to get a copy to so and so at once if he had already paid, and thought "all Irish notices ought to be sent out, as, with a new Irish Postmaster General and a vigilance committee in clerical hands you never know from one day to the next what may occur."

We managed to get some of the glue out of Joyce's hair with a "remover" we had, and all the copies of *Ulysses* safely in the hands of subscribers in England and Ireland before the authorities realized it. In the United States, Quinn and one or two other subscribers received their copies, so I got the rest off as quickly as possible. A first batch was sent over, and more were to follow, when I discovered that every copy was being confiscated at the Port of New York. I suspended shipments, and the poor subscribers waited, while I looked around for help.

Minerva-Hemingway

Now it's no secret that the hero Ulysses has friends high up, or, rather, a friend—in fact, the Goddess Minerva. She appears now in one, now in another, disguise. This time it was in the very male form of Ernest Hemingway.

I hope the following disclosures won't get Hemingway into trouble with the authorities—surely they wouldn't bother someone who is a Nobel Prize winner—but it was due to Hemingway that my copies of *Ulysses* penetrated into the United States.

I set my problem before Minerva-Hemingway. He said, "Give me twenty-four hours," and the next day he came back with a plan. I was to hear from a friend of his in Chicago, a certain Bernard B., a most obliging friend, whom I call Saint Bernard because of his rescue work, and he would let me know how the business could be carried out.

This man wrote to say that he was going ahead with his preparations and that he was moving over to Canada. He asked if I would be willing to pay the rent on a studio in Toronto, which I agreed to at once, of course. Then he sent me the address of his new domicile and told me to ship all the copies to him there. I sent them off, and, since there was no ban on *Ulysses* in Canada, they reached him safely. The job he then undertook was one requiring great courage and cunning; he had to get hundreds of these huge books across the border.

Daily, he boarded the ferry, a copy of *Ulysses* stuffed down inside his pants, as he described it to me later. It was in the days of bootlegging, so a certain number of odd-shaped characters were around, but that only increased the risk of being searched.

As the work progressed, and he was getting down to the last few dozen copies, Bernard imagined the port officials were beginning to eye him somewhat suspiciously. He was afraid they might soon inquire more closely into the real nature of the business—presumably selling his drawings—that took him back and forth every day. He found a friend who was willing to help him, and the two of them boarded the ferry daily, each with two copies now, since they had to work fast—one in front and one behind; they must have looked like a couple of paternity cases.

What a weight off our friend's mind, and off his person, when he got the last of his great tomes over to the other side!

If Joyce had foreseen all these difficulties, maybe he would have written a smaller book.

Anyhow, the *Ulysses* subscribers in America who received their copies should know that they have Hemingway and Hemingway's obliging friend to thank for that large parcel the American Express delivered at their door one day.

Meanwhile, Joyce and *Ulysses* had practically taken over the bookshop in the rue de l'Odéon. We attended to Joyce's correspondence, were his bankers, his agents, his errand boys. We made appointments for him, won friends for him, arranged all the business of the translations of his work published in Germany, Poland, Hungary, Czechoslovakia. Joyce arrived at the bookshop toward noon every day. Neither he nor his publisher bothered about lunch. He returned often in the evening, if any more business was to be transacted.

With Joyce's growing fame, more and more friends, strangers, fans, and members of the press seeking Joyce had to be encouraged, discouraged, welcomed, or treated roughly, according to the circumstances, but they all had to be dealt with at the bookshop in one way or another, and, if necessary, prevented from approaching the great man.

I was free to refuse all these services, of course, and if I accepted the Joycean job, it was because I enjoyed it immensely.

A Photograph of Mr. Bloom

From the author of *Ulysses* himself, I learned what Mr. Bloom looked like. Joyce asked me one day if I would write to Mr. Holbrook Jackson, the editor of a little review in London called *To-Day*, and ask him to send me a photograph of himself. I knew his review. It had printed an article about Adrienne Monnier's bookshop; also a friendly one on Joyce's work. Joyce didn't say that he and Jackson had ever met, but I imagine they had, perhaps on Joyce's first visit to London. Anyhow, they seemed to be interested in each other, and from some years back.

The photograph arrived. I showed it to Joyce. He scrutinized it at some length and seemed disappointed; then, handing it to me, he said: "If you want to know what Leopold Bloom looked like here is someone who resembles him. But, he went on, "the photo is not a good likeness. He doesn't look as much like Bloom in it." Anyhow, I kept the photograph carefully; it was the only one of Mr. Bloom I ever had.

"Those Scribblings of Mine"

An undated letter that Joyce must have written at the bookshop when I was out, since it is on Shakespeare and Company stationery, reads in part as follows:

Dear Miss Beach: Since you go and pay several hundred francs postage (!) on those scribblings etc of mine it is possible you may wish to have the MS of *Dubliners* so I shall give it to you when it arrives. I will sell only the dummy copy of the first edition: I think part of the *Dubliners* is Dublin work. I have also a heap of MSS in Trieste that I forgot all about until this instant about 1500 pages of the first draft for *A Portrait of the Artist* (utterly unlike the book). . . .

Can these words be still cut on the plate after (as sung by Phoblocht) Music by O. Gianni! Words by A. Hames¦

(the second exclamation [illegible] upside down)

With kindest regards
Sincerely Yours
James Joyce

The date of this letter would be January, 1922, I think, since Joyce asks if it is too late to "cut on the plate" something in *Ulysses* he wants to add. The "heap of MSS in Trieste" to which he refers included the *Stephen Hero*, what he calls the "first draft for *A Portrait of the Artist*," and "A Sketch for a

Portrait of the Artist" written in his sister Mabel's copybook, most precious to me of all his manuscripts.

Joyce gave me also the original manuscript of *Chamber Music*, the one he said he wrote on the largest, finest paper he could find to read aloud to Yeats. At least that is what he told me. It was incomplete; three of the poems were missing: Nos. 21, 35, and 36. I noted carefully that Joyce gave me this manuscript on October 5, but neglected to put down the year of this gift and the dates when he bestowed other manuscripts on me. But on the one he considered the most important, the sketch for *A Portrait of the Artist*, he wrote an inscription with the date and a description of his gift.

Joyce had noticed that I treasured the least scrap of his handwriting. No doubt he thought no one would appreciate the gift of them as much as myself; and I believe he was right.

Shakespeare and Company Regrets . . .

Joyce was soon deriving a steady income from *Ulysses* in spite of the fact that it was denied its normal outlets in the English-speaking countries. And, of course, its reputation as a banned book helped the sales. It was saddening, however, to see such a work listed in catalogues of erotica alongside *Fanny Hill*, *The Perfumed Garden*, and that everlasting Casanova, not to speak of plain pornography like *Raped on the Rail*. An Irish priest, purchasing *Ulysses*, asked me, "Any other spicy books?"

Many fine writers have produced erotica, and a few of them, Baudelaire and Verlaine, for instance, have even succeeded in making the subject interesting. John Cleland settled all his debts with his amusing as well as profitable *Fanny Hill*. Joyce, needless to say, had no such purpose in writing *Ulysses*. He was no specialist, but a general practitioner—all the parts of the body come into *Ulysses*. As he himself said plaintively, "There is less than ten per cent of *that* in my book."

After the success of *Ulysses*, writers flocked to Shakespeare and Company on the assumption that I was going to specialize in erotica. They brought me their most erotic efforts. And not only that; they insisted on reading me passages that couldn't, they thought, fail to tempt a person with my supposed tastes. For instance, there was the small man with whiskers who drove up to the bookshop in a carriage—a barouche and pair hired for the occasion to impress me, as he afterward confessed. His long arms swinging apelike in front of him, he walked into the shop, deposited on my table a parcel that had the look of a manuscript, and introduced himself as Frank Harris. I had liked his book *The Man Shakespeare*. I had also liked the volume on Wilde, and especially Shaw's preface about Wilde's gigantism. So had Joyce. I asked Harris what his manuscript was about. He undid the parcel and showed me a thing called *My Life and Loves*, which he assured me went much further than Joyce. He claimed he was really the only English writer who had got "under a woman's skin."

Frank Harris's stories about Wilde were beginning, at that time, to show a good deal of wear and tear and, like Wilde's, were more or less borrowed. Then the venereal diseases of English statesmen didn't matter much to me, either. Harris had a pleasant way of reading poetry, and when he gave up trying to make me listen to *My Life and Loves* and took *Songs of Sunrise* from the shelf and read a few lines of that, he was quite endearing. But I never could see how a man who had had the good taste to marry a charming woman like Nellie Harris could fall so low as to produce *My Life and Loves*.

I suggested that he try Jack Kahane, who was always looking for "hot books," and *My Life and Loves* found a happy home at the Obelisk Press.

Though he was disappointed in me as a result of my lack of enthusiasm for his memoirs, Frank Harris continued to be friendly. I persuaded Joyce to accept his invitation to lunch at the Chatham, a hotel much frequented by the English, which used to be famous for its cuisine and cellar. The only other guest was an English newspaper friend of Harris's. Joyce suspected Harris and his pal of a plot to trap him into an interview—he always shunned interviewers—and hardly opened his mouth all through lunch. To the spicy tales of Harris and his friend, Joyce was totally unresponsive.

It was wicked of me, but I couldn't resist the temptation to play a little trick on Frank Harris. Once, when he was rushing to catch a train to Nice, he stopped at the bookshop for something to read on the long journey. Could I suggest something exciting? My eye wandered along the shelf where I kept a few Tauchnitz volumes. I asked him if he had read *Little Women*. He jumped at the title, which to someone with an obsession like his could have only the French meaning of *petites femmes*. He grabbed the two volumes of Louisa Alcott's "hot book" and off he dashed to the station.

I was filled with remorse the next time I saw him. He didn't mention the hoax, but he, who was always so pleasant, was visibly resentful, and I saw the wickedness of my ways.

The next book I was obliged to turn down was *Lady Chatterley's Lover*. I didn't admire this work, which I found the least interesting of its author's productions, but it was very hard to refuse Lawrence's appeal to come to its rescue.

The situation of *Lady Chatterley's Lover* was desperate, according to two of Lawrence's friends who came to ask me to take over its publication. One of them, Richard Aldington, I knew already; Aldous Huxley and I now met for the first time. He was tall and had to stoop as we went under the low doorway into the back room to discuss his mission. He was making a sacrifice for his friend D. H. Lawrence, I thought, in condescending to come to the headquarters of James Joyce, to whose *Ulysses* he was not friendly. *Lady Chatterley* had already appeared in Florence, in a limited edition issued by Messrs. Davis and Orioli, that charming Anglo-Italian couple whose names were well known to connoisseurs of fine editions.

Unfortunately, *Lady Chatterley*, like *Ulysses* and other exiled books, was not protected by copyright. Pirates had pounced on it, and an apparently unlimited, inexpensive, and unauthorized edition was circulating in Paris without any profit whatsoever to the author. Lawrence was anxious to have me publish the book in a cheap edition in Paris and put an end to the pirating.

His friends' visits having proved unsuccessful, Lawrence himself came to see me. He was brought to the bookshop by a mutual friend, Miss Beveridge, an English artist who had been his neighbor in Sicily. He noticed the reproduction of her portrait of him at Shakespeare and Company and signed it for me. Also he said he would like me to have his photograph by Stieglitz and would ask him to send one.

A tall blonde woman, Mrs. Frieda Lawrence, accompanied her husband on his subsequent visits, but she looked at the books while he and I discussed his business, so, to my regret, she and I hardly exchanged a word.

D. H. Lawrence was a man of great personal charm. It was always a matter of wonder to me why a writer so greatly gifted never seemed to have the power to produce what his readers were expecting of him. As a man he was very interesting— fascinating. I could understand the devotion of Lawrence's friends, and why women pursued him across countries and over the seas.

It was sad refusing Lawrence's *Lady*, particularly because he was so ill the last time I saw him that he had got out of bed to come to the bookshop and had a flushed, feverish look. It was distressing trying to explain my reasons for not undertaking other publications than *Ulysses*: lack of capital—but you couldn't persuade anyone that Shakespeare and Company hadn't made a fortune—and that we lacked space, personnel, and time. It was difficult to tell him that I didn't want to get a name as a publisher of erotica, and impossible to say that I wanted to be a one-book publisher—what could anybody offer after *Ulysses*?

Lawrence wrote to me to ask again whether I had changed my mind, and I replied to the address he gave me in the south of France. But since he says in one of his published letters that he never heard from me, I suppose my reply didn't reach him.

My friend and Joyce's, Mr. Frank Budgen, was present at Lawrence's funeral in Vence, and sent me some snapshots of the temporary grave showing, on the wall above it, the Lawrence "Phoenix" of which, now that he has been transferred to Taos, all traces seem to have disappeared. I think a plate should mark the spot of his first resting place.

Hardly a day passed without another visitor bringing his manuscript and sometimes a backer, who, in the case of Aleicester Crowley, was a blonde lady, aggressively partisan.

Aleicester (pronounced Alester) Crowley was as peculiar as he sounded in the tales told of him, and, of course, in his own *Diary of a Drugfiend*. His clay-colored head was bald except for a single strand of black hair stretching from his forehead over the top of his head and down to the nape of his neck. The strand seemed glued to the skin so that it was not likely to blow up in the wind. A self-mummified-looking man, he was rather repulsive. My acquaintance with him was brief. I wondered, looking at him, whether what some of my English friends hinted was true—that he was in the Intelligence Service. I thought someone less conspicuous might have been chosen.

The monks in the monastery on Mount Athos, Black Masses, and so on—all of these were in Crowley's books. The billygoat and the Oxford student, I hope, were inventions of others; he never mentioned them.

It was quite alarming to see the blonde lady open a portfolio and produce a prospectus announcing the "Forthcoming *Memoirs of Aleicester Crowley*" under my imprint and the draft of a contract with Shakespeare and Company requiring only a signature. Everything had been taken care of in advance, even to the provision that Shakespeare and Company turn over 50 per cent of the book's earnings to Mr. Crowley, and give him our mailing list as well!

One morning a boy with "Maxim's" on his cap got off his bicycle at the door of the bookshop and handed me a note. It was from the headwaiter of that famous establishment, and it announced that he would like to submit his memoirs to my firm. He had known everybody who was anybody in his time— crowned heads, stage celebrities, *grandes cocottes*, statesmen. He could tell such stories! This was likely to be the most exciting event the literary world had seen in a long time— surpassing, it was hinted, *Ulysses*. He hoped Shakespeare and Company wouldn't let such a chance escape.

Then, about that time, I got a letter from someone representing Miss Tallulah Bankhead, asking if her memoirs would interest me for publication. Miss Bankhead must have been precocious; she could hardly have been more than a child at the date of that letter. The Bankhead manuscript never turned up, but if I had been allowed to have a look at it, I don't think I could have turned it down.

The fact was, however, that I was so busy with my bookshop and my one-author publishing business and looking after all the little reviews and co-operating with the new little publishing houses that were springing up around me that-it would have been a real mishap to any manuscript to have been accepted by Shakespeare and Company.

Second Edition

Not long after *Ulysses* was published, Miss Weaver wrote to me and asked my consent to have plates made from the type of the first edition, at her expense. I gave it immediately, though I was somewhat surprised at this precipitate second edition. I could not refuse anything to Joyce's benefactress, and, besides, I knew the plan was Joyce's. He had dashed over to London shortly after *Ulysses* came out and had arranged the whole business, with his usual haste, while I was trying to overcome

the difficulties of delivering copies of the first edition to subscribers in the United States—with the help, as I have already
related, of my "best customer." Joyce had protested when I
told him that I was printing a thousand copies. "That dull
book," he said, "you won't sell a copy of it." But when he saw
that, on the contrary, the edition of a thousand wasn't nearly
enough to satisfy the demands for it, he must have regretted
that it wasn't larger. And hearing of the high price copies were
fetching, he decided that a fresh supply would put a stop to
speculation and that the author, rather than the speculators,
would get the profits. *Ulysses* was his big investment, and it
was natural that he should try to get as much out of it as he
could.

The second edition, like the first, was printed in Dijon. It
closely resembled the first in format, and it also had a blue
cover, but it carried the notation: "Published by John Rodker
for the Egoist Press." Two thousand copies were printed. A
part of the edition was shipped to Dover, where the copies
were seized and promptly burned in "the King's Chimney"—
according to Miss Weaver, that was the expression used. She
told me that on hearing of the seizure she had rushed to Dover
only to find that her copies of *Ulysses* had gone up in smoke.
The copies that were dispatched to the United States also
perished, probably drowned like so many kittens in New York
Harbor. But some of them must have swum to shore, and,
judging by the letters I received from time to time, the
similarity of the two editions was the cause of some confusion.
Meanwhile, I received a great many complaints from Paris
booksellers, who, on hearing of this second edition appearing a
few months after the first, were indignant over what they considered a transgression against the rules governing limited editions. They blamed me, of course, though the second edition
was not my publication.

It was indeed my fault, and I thought their complaints
justified. It was due to my inexperience, and I should have
thought of the booksellers who had not been given enough

time to get rid of their stock of the original limited edition before another one was announced. Apparently Miss Weaver and Joyce saw nothing strange in this procedure, for it seems that in a letter to Miss Weaver, Joyce expressed surprise at having heard from Miss Beach that the Paris booksellers were complaining.

The fate of the second edition made it clear that all efforts to bring out *Ulysses* in England were for the present useless; and that there was no hope of getting it published in my country, either, until someone suppressed the Society for the Suppression of Vice. So, after its attempt to skip over the Channel and the ocean, Shakespeare and Company's "lost one" returned to the rue de l'Odéon.

Ulysses Settles Down

The Shakespeare and Company edition went through printing after printing—*Ulysses* IV, V, VI, VII, and so on. Joyce said it reminded him of the Popes. (And speaking of Popes, a young man who had stopped at the bookshop to pick up a copy on his way to Rome, wrote me that the Pope had unwittingly blessed *Ulysses*. He said that in an audience at the Vatican he had carried the book concealed under his coat.) Some of the printings, to Joyce's dismay, were in white jackets, like waiters, because they had run out of the blue covers at Dijon. Some, for the sake of economy, were printed on a sort of blotting paper.

For *Ulysses* VIII, I had the type reset, and the errors I had apologized for in *Ulysses* I were removed. Or so we thought. I believe it was Frank Harris who recommended that we have the proofs read by a friend of his on the *Daily Mail*. This man, who was an expert proofreader, went through them carefully several times. I went over them, too, but, since I am no expert, that didn't mean anything. This eighth printing arrived, and I put a copy of it in Joyce's hand. He eagerly scrutinized the first pages with the help of his two pairs of glasses plus a magnifying glass—and I heard an exclamation. Three errors already!

In spite of its typographical errors, *Ulysses* sold very well, mainly at first to the big English and American bookshops on the Right Bank. As its fame grew, all the French bookshops, whether or not they had ever sold English books before, discovered *Ulysses*—so great was the demand for it. Men from places all over town who were sent to fetch our publication used to assemble in the bookshop, and their conversations, usually on the subject of books and, naturally, concerned mainly with their weight, interested me a great deal. I regretted that my publication was so heavy; they admired me as the publisher of a best seller. They would spread their squares of green cloth on the floor, place perhaps twenty copies of *Ulysses* on the cloth, tie the four corners into a knot, and sling the heavy bundle over their shoulders. Then they would go on to pick up other books. It was a job that obliged them to drop in frequently at a bistrot to quench their thirst. One of these friends used to burst in demanding loudly: "*Un Joylisse.*" Once an order was handed me for "I Lily by James Joyce."

We sent copies to India, China, and Japan, had customers in the Straits Settlements and, I daresay, among the head-hunters of Sarawak. Those sold directly to American or English customers in the bookshop were disguised, if requested, as *Shakespeare's Works Complete in One Volume* or *Merry Tales for Little Folks* or other volumes of the right size and with suitable jackets. Tourists developed quite a technique in smuggling *Ulysses* into the United States. It was more difficult to get it into England.

Brisk though sales were in Paris, the book would have brought the author and the publisher a great deal more money if it had not been cut off from its normal market in English-speaking countries. Its outlet in non-English-speaking countries was limited.

ELEVEN

Bryher

Bryher, Bryher. I wondered if the owner of this interesting name would ever come to my bookshop. I already knew her husband, Robert McAlmon, but Bryher disliked cities—those "rows of shops," as she called them. She shunned crowds, was no frequenter of cafés, and was very retiring. Still, I knew that she loved Paris and everything in France, and I hoped that she would consent to overlook the fact that my shop was one of those in the hateful "rows."

Then, one day, a great day for Shakespeare and Company, Robert McAlmon brought her in—a shy young English girl in a tailor-made suit and a hat with a couple of streamers that reminded me of a sailor's. I couldn't keep my eyes off Bryher's: they were so blue—bluer than the sea or sky or even the Blue Grotto in Capri. More beautiful still was the expression in Bryher's eyes. I'm afraid that to this day I stare at her eyes.

Bryher, as far as I can remember, never said a word. She was practically soundless, a not uncommon thing in England; no small talk whatsoever—the French call it "letting the others pay the expenses of the conversation." So McAlmon and I did the talking, and Bryher did the looking. She was quietly observing everything in her Bryhery way, just as she observed everything when she visited "The Warming Pan" teashop in the London blitz days—and, as *Beowulf* proves, nothing escaped her.

This was so different from the way most people blew in and out, wrapped up in themselves like parcels for the post.

Bryher's interest in Shakespeare and Company was real—and protective. And her interest and protection have continued from that day.

Bryher's name is that of one of the Scilly Isles, where she used to spend her holidays as a child. Though her friends never call her anything but Bryher, her family and everyone who knew her when she was a little girl call her Winifred—her full name, I believe, is Annie Winifred. She was the daughter of Sir John Ellerman, a giant in finance and one of the most remarkable men in the England of George V. Among other things, he was an outstanding Alpine climber in his youth.

Little Winifred's parents were very fond of her, but, at the same time, puzzled by her strange character. She hated being dressed up in pretty frocks and sashes like other little girls, and having her hair curled. And oh! those petticoats, layers of them, and a flannel one in winter! Instead of those interesting doings in *The Cat of Bubastes* and her sea stories and histories, she had to put up with governesses escorting her, and interminable meals served by a man in white gloves! If only those kind parents of hers had guessed that their child was planning to run away to sea, that a little "Tom Sawyer" was only waiting for the first chance to jump out of the window!

Bryher has written about her first visit to Paris, with her father and mother, in a small volume entitled *Paris 1900*. They brought her to the famous Exposition. She was five, and small for her age. She was also a fierce little Britisher, who wanted to punch a Frenchman in the eye when he made some remark about her country and *"les Böers"*—it was at the time of the Boer War.

She was not much older when her parents took her to Egypt. There the child was fascinated by hieroglyphics, and found

Egyptian stories far more entertaining than those about the cat and the dog in the primers other children were spelling out. Cairo was fun. One day, when her parents went off on camels and left her at home, she pulled all the sheets and pillowcases off the beds and dressed up in them. She so frightened the servants, when she appeared before them— they took her for a ghost—that they ran screaming away, and not a servant remained in the hotel.

The misunderstanding between Bryher and her family increased as she grew up. In her autobiographical novel, *Development*, one of a series that takes her up to her marriage, she tells of her tragic failure to adapt herself to a life she didn't fit into. She was only happy at her fencing lessons, and, of course, when she was reading. In her early teens, Henty and the sea stories were replaced by French poetry, and Mallarmé became Bryher's hero.

Through poetry, Bryher escaped at last from surroundings that were her despair. Then she met Hilda Doolittle, who was to become her lifelong friend, and, through H. D., entered her own world, that of writers. H. D. was one of the most admired of the so-called Imagists, a group that included Ezra Pound, John Gould Fletcher, and others, all of whom were gathered in London in those years.

Since Bryher's best friend was an American, she began to take a great interest in our country, and decided she would visit it. So Bryher and her native guide, H. D., went "out to the States," as Bryher always puts it.

The principal event of this trip for Bryher, aside from meeting Marianne Moore and other poets for the first time, was her marriage to the young writer from Minnesota, Robert McAlmon. They were married the day after they met. Bryher did not tell the man she married who she was. Such was her dread of opposition to her plans for emancipation that she intended to keep her marriage a secret from her parents until she could take her husband to England and introduce him to them,

when it would be too late for them to oppose it. But the newspapers had the story, and the very next day McAlmon learned
that he had married the daughter of Sir John Ellerman.

Bryher's parents took the news very well indeed, and they
quite liked their son-in-law. The whole family, including
Bryher's young brother, John, took Robert to their hearts,
twang and all.

Bryher preferred to keep away from "crowds" and cities.
McAlmon's days were mostly spent in Paris, in the cafés of the
Left Bank, among his writing friends. His talents made him one
of the most interesting personalities of the twenties. His ample
means, unique in his Bohemian world, contributed not a little
to his popularity. The drinks were always on him, and alas!
often in him. With the funds now at his command, Robert
became a publisher. In his Contact Editions he brought out
some very successful books. McAlmon was much liked by his
friends, but he was too intolerant of restraint, personal or literary. As he himself said to me, "I'm only a drinker."

Bryher seldom came to Paris, though we managed to lure
her there once in a while—perhaps as often as once a year.
When she did come, there was great rejoicing, and Adrienne
would invite some of our French friends to meet her. On one
of her visits to my bookshop, she saw the Shakespeare customers rooting around among the pile of letters on the mantelpiece in search of their mail. Shakespeare and Company was
the American Express of the artists on the Left Bank. We did
banking, too, sometimes, and I used to call the shop "The
Left Bank." Bryher thought our important postal service should
have its box, and thenceforth a fine, large sort of case, with
pigeonholes marked with the letters of the alphabet, made
distribution of all that mail a pleasure.

The most appreciated gift to Shakespeare and Company was
the bust of our Patron Saint, William Shakespeare, in colored
Staffordshire ware, which Lady Ellerman picked up for us
in Brighton. From the day Bob McAlmon arrived from London carrying a parcel wrapped up in newspapers and set up this

offering on the mantelpiece, it remained our most valued ornament. I always felt it brought us good luck.

Bryher, though she won't like my mentioning it, has done more than anyone knows to maintain international contacts throughout wars, and to keep together her large family of intellectuals, who are dispersed in many countries. She has looked after them in war and peace, and her correspondence is vast.

Bryher would hate the word "philanthropy," but I am hard put to find another for some of the things she has done for people in trouble. For instance, one of her most extraordinary feats in this line was the rescue of dozens of Nazi victims. I was a witness to her maneuverings to get them away from their persecutors and finally across the sea to the United States, and to her care of them until they got established in the New World. What a historic tale Bryher's whole life would make. Fortunately, she is now telling it.

TWELVE

Variety

Life at Shakespeare and Company was rather tumultuous for a person who liked to be left alone in a corner to dream and read and meditate. Some people retire from their activities to a life of contemplation. With me it was the contrary: first the musing, then the bustling. "You are the perfect type of extrovert," observed a pupil of Freud's just arrived from Vienna.

There was, first of all, the regular routine of a bookshop. There's a great deal to do in a bookshop. As in the "Rhyme of the Nancy Bell," I was both "the cook and the captain bold." I was a combination of apprentice, boss, and personnel —until Myrsine came to help me. Imagine, too, the bookkeeping, besides the bookselling and lending! I had to run three bank accounts in three different currencies, American, French, and English, and calculating in tuppences and centimes and pennies was one of my most puzzling occupations. My peculiar arithmetic made it rather hard for someone in business. I lost a good deal of time and wasted large sheets of paper that way. Once, I happened to mention my difficulties to my old Princeton friend Jessie Sayre, Woodrow Wilson's beautiful second daughter, who was stopping in Paris and took a great deal of interest in my bookshop. Jessie suggested that I come to her hotel one evening and she would soon teach me arithmetic by a system that had been very successful with a class of backward children she had taught. After dinner, we retired to her room and set to work. The Sayres—her husband, strange to say, had a striking resemblance to her father—left Paris the next day. Jessie went away convinced that I had immediately caught on, thanks to her system. I didn't want to disillusion such a good friend, and, besides, I was too much ashamed of myself, so I never told her that I went right back to my large-page calculation.

Adrienne Monnier's bookshop gave one the impression of peacefulness; you slowed down as soon as you entered it. But, then, Adrienne hadn't a Joyce on the premises. Besides, we Americans are a boisterous people. Shakespeare and Company was boisterous. "Variety Beach," my father's nickname among his classmates at Princeton, fitted his daughter in her bookshop in Paris.

From 9 o'clock, when dear M. Huchon, Anglo-Saxon professor at the Sorbonne, came to get a light novel for his English wife, till any hour up to midnight, students, readers, writers, translators, publishers, publishers' travelers, and just friends were in and out. Among the members of the lending library were a great many writers of the day, and, of course, there were all their anonymous friends who read them. I was particularly fond of those who demanded Joyce and Eliot, but the others had their rights respected. I supplied the whole "Bindle" series to the mother of seven chirping little ones, and even produced Charles Morgan when the French insisted on him. I was very fond of plain readers like myself. What would the writers do without us? And the bookshops?

Fitting people with books is about as difficult as fitting them with shoes. We had customers ordering the oddest things from the United States or England—for instance, that one who came once a year to get his *Raphael's Ephemerides*. Why didn't they simply buy *A Boy's Will* instead of asking for something I didn't have in stock?

Half of my customers were, of course, French, and my work included giving informal courses in American literature to bring them up to date. I found that many of them hadn't heard of our new writers.

One of my "bunnies" was a Baconian, and the name of my bookshop riled him so much that he couldn't keep away from it. After gulping down his breakfast of bacon and eggs, he would hurry to Shakespeare and Company and do his best to prevent me from answering all my piled-up business letters addressed to Shakespeare and Company. He would jerk the *Anatomy of Melancholy* or some other volume off the shelves and leave it open at the page that proved that Bacon was Shakespeare's ghost. This "bunny" was really violent. One day I noticed he was eying the poker. He had decided, no doubt, to lay out the proprietor of Shakespeare and Company on the floor of her premises, and I was quite relieved when Hemingway dropped in for his morning visit.

I preferred my children "bunnies." They came right in and sat down in a long-suffering little armchair at a round red table to read Bryher's *Geography*. Bryher thought books should be big and flat so you could sit on them. I was always glad to interrupt less important business to show these members Larbaud's West Pointers and all my toys on top of the cupboard in the back room; they had to be lifted up to see them.

One of my favorites was Harriet Waterfield. Her father, Gordon Waterfield, was writing a book about his ancestress Lady Duff Gordon: a most interesting biography, which I can recommend to anyone who hasn't already read this absorbing story.

Harriet was five. She said to her mother, "You know Sylvia Beach is my best friend." I felt the same way about Harriet Waterfield. She took me to the zoo in the Bois de Boulogne one day when we should have been attending to our business at the bookshop. It was spring, and the animal small fry were wandering around and getting under foot. It was rather annoying when they jumped up on you and chewed the buttons off your best coat—your mother had said not to spoil it. It was a great relief to meet the elephants, who were not the jumping-up kind of animals. Harriet said: "Next time let's go stwaight to the elephants."

A little fair-haired girl in a white dress came into the bookshop one day with her father, and sat down at the small red table to look at the children's books. This child was Violaine, godchild of Claudel and named after the heroine in his play *La Jeune Fille Violaine*. Her father, the poet and ambassador Henri Hoppenot, was one of our best friends. Violaine and her mother, Hélène Hoppenot, and her father were just back from Peking.

This little girl, who knew English almost better than French and was deep in Kate Greenaway that day while I talked with her father, was, at twenty, the heroine of the most dangerous exploits of the Resistance.

There was also a sprinkling of dog members at Shakespeare and Company, and they were not always welcomed with politeness by my dog, Teddy.

About this dog, Teddy. He belonged originally to one of my customers, an attractive young woman from Brooklyn. He was a wire-haired terrier with some mongrel blood, and a dog of great charm. He came often to the bookshop with his Brooklyn license, which he would let no one remove. Then one day his mistress told me that, fond as she was of Teddy, she could not keep him any longer, and asked me to accept him as a present. I told her that I couldn't keep a dog and a James Joyce and a bookshop. Well, then, she said, Teddy would have to be put to sleep.

So I agreed to take Teddy on trial, to stay only if he was acceptable to Mousse, the big shaggy shepherd dog at Adrienne Monnier's parents' place in the country, where we spent weekends. With this understanding, Teddy's mistress handed him over along with his leash and detailed instructions about his health, his diet (to the amazement of the Monniers, it laid stress on canned salmon), his behavior, his tricks, which she had taken much trouble to teach him, and his vocabulary. Teddy's tricks delighted many a child and would have got him a job in a circus any time he needed to earn his living. He turned around and around on his toes, lay flat on the ground till you counted to "*Three!*" balanced a stick on his nose, tossed it and caught it as it fell.

I feared the transfer to another mistress would be a blow to Teddy. He not only accepted his new partner, but the first time his former mistress came back to the bookshop, he didn't even bother to get up to speak to her. Probably pride.

The following weekend, as Adrienne, Teddy, and I were going through the gate to catch our train, the attendant stopped us. "You can't take that dog," he said; "not without a muzzle." We had no muzzle and no time to get one, and this train was the last one we could get. Adrienne, who was never at a loss, got out a big handkerchief and tied it around Teddy's jaws. And before the man could think of what to say, we dashed off, boarded the train, and were on our way to the country.

Mousse was a mountain dog that I had brought, as a puppy, from Savoy to Adrienne's father. No one, not even his master, could take the liberty of brushing Mousse's coat—a mountain dog would never submit to such an outrage to his dignity. Once, only once, Adrienne's mother tried to comb his tangled locks. Mousse seized the comb, extracted the hair that had been taken from him, and swallowed it.

We were sure that Mousse wouldn't see the need of a Teddy. But, after a first fierce encounter, the two dogs became friends, Mousse admiring Teddy, an intellectual; Teddy looking up to Mousse, a real he-dog.

Adrienne thought Teddy highly evolved; he had passed through many metamorphoses, or, as Molly Bloom would say, "met-him-pike-hoses." Adrienne thought that in his next reincarnation he would be a postman: since Adrienne's father had been in the Postal Service, this remark showed her esteem for Teddy. I liked him in his present dog stage, and he liked me— I'm sure he would have laid down his dog's life for me.

1   Sylvia Beach at Shakespeare and Company, 8 rue Dupuytren

2   Sylvia Beach and Holly Beach

3   *Adrienne Monnier in front of Shakespeare and Company*

4　*Ezra Pound,*
John Quinn,
Ford Madox Ford,
and James Joyce

5　*T. S. Eliot*

6 Bryher

7 H. D.

8 Djuna Barnes

9 Paul Valéry

11 *Adrienne Monnier in her bookshop*

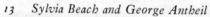

13 *Sylvia Beach and George Antheil*

12 *Adrienne Monnier*

10 *Sylvia Beach
in her bookshop*
(OPPOSITE PAGE)

14   *John Rodker, James Joyce, Sylvia Beach, and Cyprian Beach*

15   *James Joyce at Bognor*

16   "*Mr. Bloom*"

17   *Sylvia Beach and James Joyce*

18   *Harriet Weaver*

19   *Ben W. Huebsch*

20 *James Joyce at home*   21 *James Joyce and his daughter, Lucia*

22 *James Joyce and Eugene Jolas*

23 *Sylvia Beach*

24 *Allen Tate*

26 *George Antheil*

25 *Thornton Wilder*

27 Scott Fitzgerald
    and Adrienne Monnier

28 Robert McAlmon

29 Ezra Pound

30 William Bird

31 Ernest Hemingway

32 Robert McAlmon
and Ernest Hemingway

33 Janet Flanner

34 Archibald MacLeish

35 *Valery Larbaud*

36 *Léon-Paul Fargue and Sylvia Beach*

37 *André Gide*

38   *Alice B. Toklas and Gertrude Stein*

39   *Stuart Gilbert*

Of course, whenever Joyce came to the bookshop I had to hurry Teddy out of the way. Poor Joyce! He didn't like it when Adrienne and I got a car—he thought only officials should be allowed to use them—and now here was this "feerrce dog" at Shakespeare and Company.

Joyce had no use for Teddy, but he thoroughly approved of the Shakespeare and Company cat, a black-as-ink cat named Lucky. Joyce never wore gloves, so Lucky's appetite for the fingers of them didn't annoy him as it did people who had laid down a good pair on one of the tables and found them with the fingers devoured. You couldn't make Lucky see how wrong this was. All I could do was to put up a sign warning the customers of the danger to gloves. To hats, too; I was very much ashamed of Lucky when he plowed up the crown of a very fine new hat of Hemingway's. Also there was the time when friends came to tea at Adrienne's, and Lucky chewed the fingers off all the gloves in the bedroom. Mrs. Joyce was in hysterics about somebody else's gloves. She didn't discover till after leaving that she, too, was a victim.

Visitors and Friends

Visitors from all countries dropped in at Shakespeare and Company, and in the early twenties a customer turned up from what was then called Russia—Serge Eisenstein, a great artist and a man full of exciting ideas on the subject of films. He was certainly one of the most interesting men I have ever met. Eisenstein followed the literary movement closely and was an ardent admirer of Joyce. He would have liked to make a film from *Ulysses*, but he had too much respect for the text, he told me, to sacrifice it for the sake of the picture.

Eisenstein was back in Paris later. He invited Adrienne and me to the Russian Embassy, where he showed us his new picture, *The General Line*, and told us some of his ideas on the subject. He had so many ideas that he could never express half of them in any given time—nor perhaps finish a picture within any time limit.

I made an arrangement with Eisenstein to supply him with the new books in English in return for contemporary Russian writing. Judging by what he sent me, nothing particularly important seemed to be appearing in Russia at the time; or perhaps it was the translations that were lacking.

The whole Litvinov family also visited the bookshop. Mrs. Ivy Litvinov was English, and her husband was almost an Irishman, since he had attended the same university as Joyce in Dublin. Photographs of the Litvinov children were added to those of my other young customers; Tania I remember particularly.

My customers and friends included a Chinese professor of phonetics (with twins), Cambodians, Greeks, Hindus, Central Europeans, and South Americans. But most of them, of course, were American or French or English.

Janet Flanner, who later adopted the pen name of Genêt, was one of my earliest American friends. She was in and out of the bookshop very often in the twenties. Once, she stopped for a minute in a taxi on her way to her train to Rome, just to take the trouble to make the Shakespeare and Company library a present of two superb art books. Adrienne Monnier borrowed these volumes and was so fond of gazing at the illustrations that it was some time before she was willing to part with them.

Janet Flanner was always off, either to London or to Rome or to some other place to which her career as a roving writer took her. She was brilliant. She was also a great worker. But she always found time to look after people, as I can testify. Once, as a small return for one of her kindnesses, I presented her with a copy of *Ulysses* with a little manuscript of the author in it. Some years later, when Joyce values were mounting, she asked me if I had any objection to her selling her copy to a famous library, I, not she, to benefit from the sale. That's Janet Flanner.

I thought a *Life* photographer had a good idea, at the time of the Liberation in 1944, when he photographed two of my old customers at No. 12, rue de l'Odéon: Janet Flanner and Ernest Hemingway.

Another friend who belonged to the early period was John Dos Passos. He always seemed to be on the go. I met him between *Three Soldiers* and *Manhattan Transfer*, but caught only glimpses of him as he raced by. I used to see him with Hemingway at times. One day when I opened the bookshop after the noon closing, I noticed something had been slipped under the door: a photograph of John Dos Passos. I had told Dos, as we called him, that he must bring me one for my portrait gallery.

Thornton Wilder appeared at Shakespeare and Company about the same time as Hemingway. He used to see a good deal of the young Hemingways, and came often to the bookshop. His manners were the best of any of my friends': he was rather shy and a little like a young curate; his background seemed quite different from that of others of his generation in Paris. I liked his *Cabala* and, later, his *Bridge of San Luis Rey*, and thought him very modest in spite of his achievements and his success. The French admire his *Bridge*, and might almost claim it as theirs, so much is it in the French tradition. The contrast between some of my friends in the twenties, for instance, Wilder and McAlmon, was really inexplicable unless you remember the contrasts and variety in our vast country.

After a while, I noticed with regret, because I was always fond of Thornton Wilder, and admired him, that he seemed more or less to disappear from the rue de l'Odéon in the direction of the rue Christine. Yet I never felt the slightest cooling off of our friendship. He just had business that took him elsewhere. Sherwood Anderson, too, went rather Christine-wards, that is, Steinwards.

The artist Man Ray and his pupil Berenice Abbott, who assisted him for a while, were the official portraitists of "the

Crowd." The walls of my bookshop were covered with their photographs. To be "done" by Man Ray and Berenice Abbott meant you were rated as somebody. Man Ray's photography was not, however, I imagine, what interested him most. He already had a name among the artists in the advanced movement and was a member of the Dada and Surrealist groups.

In April 1924, the booksellers and publishers in the United States noticed an article in *Publishers' Weekly* about Shakespeare and Company and were so interested by it that they usually took in my bookshop on their visits to Paris. We were proud of having caught the eye of this official organ. The author of the article was Morrill Cody, who wrote the book on that most important character, Jimmy the Barman, with an introduction by Ernest Hemingway. Like my other friends of the Paris twenties, Morrill Cody has gone far since those days, has rendered and is rendering great services to our cultural relations with France.

"The Crowd"

Djuna Barnes, so charming, so Irish, and so gifted, came to Paris early in the twenties. She belonged to the *Little Review* and Greenwich Village group, and was a friend of McAlmon's. Her first novel, which was published in 1922 and called simply, and so characteristically, *A Book*, established her as a writer. Her work, with its strangeness and its melancholy note—which contrasted with her delightful smile—did not resemble that of any other writer of the time. Moreover, she was not one to cry her wares. Fortunately, T. S. Eliot, with his usual discernment, sought her out and ushered her to the place she deserves to occupy. Even so, she doesn't seem to have been given her due in books on writers of the period. Certainly she was one of the most talented and, I think, one of the most fascinating literary figures in the Paris of the twenties.

An American artist who was around the Quarter in the first years of my bookshop was Marsden Hartley, an interesting fellow, whose *Twenty-five Poems* was published by McAlmon in his Contact Editions. He was not one of those who stayed long in Paris, but in the few glimpses I had of him I found him attractive, though perhaps a little melancholy.

Mary Butts, who bounced in and out and was a personality in the Paris of the twenties with her red cheeks and red hair, wasn't melancholy at all, at least when I saw her. Cocteau's drawing of the authoress of *Traps for Unbelievers* is quite the Mary Butts of those days. But her life was tragic, and her work, which was so promising, was interrupted suddenly by her death. All of her books that had appeared disappeared, too; they seemed to go out of print after she died, although a certain number of her novels had been published—one of them was *Ashe of Rings*—in the Contact Editions. There was also a book on Cleopatra, whom Mary Butts saw as an intellectual, almost a bluestocking.

We had three raving beauties in "the Crowd," all in one family, which was not fair. Mina Loy, the poetess, and her daughters, Joella and Faby (but that is the wrong spelling of it, no doubt), were so lovely that they were stared at wherever they went, and were used to it. But I believe if a vote had been taken, Mina would have been elected the most beautiful of the three. Joyce, who could see as well as anyone when he wanted to, observed that Joella was a beauty according to all the standards: her golden hair, her eyes, her complexion, her manners. So she had Joyce's vote. Faby, still a little girl, but beautiful, was very interesting looking. One couldn't keep one's eyes off her.

When you went to Mina's apartment you threaded your way past lamp shades that were everywhere: she made them to support her children. She made all her own clothes, also, and perhaps theirs. Her hats were very like her lamp shades; or perhaps it was the lamp shades that were like hats.

She wrote poetry whenever she had time. McAlmon brought

out a little volume of her poems with the typically Mina Loyan title *Lunar Baedecker*. (Note the misspelling of "Baedeker"— McAlmon's.)

McAlmon had a Japanese friend among our Left Bank crowd —Ken Sato, whose *Quaint Stories* McAlmon also published. The English in which these fairy stories about the fierce Samurai warriors and their boys were written was almost quainter than the tales of Gide's forerunners in Japan.

One of the people who always took a great interest in my bookshop and also in Adrienne's was my compatriot Miss Natalie Clifford Barney, the *"Amazone"* of Rémy de Gourmont's *Letters*. She rode horseback in the Bois de Boulogne every morning, hence the name. She wrote poetry, and her *salon* was famous in the Paris literary world, but I wonder if she ever took literary things very seriously. As an amazon, Miss Barney was not belligerent. On the contrary, she was charming, and, all dressed in white and with her blond coloring, most attractive. Many of her sex found her fatally so, I believe. Miss Barney was at home on Fridays at her *pavillon* in the rue Jacob, where Ninon de Lenclos had been "at home" in the seventeenth century, but I don't know whether it was on Fridays. Rémy de Gourmont was gone, but his brother was always to be seen at Miss Barney's. Her writers were mostly those of the *Mercure de France*, and perhaps that is how she fell in with Ezra Pound, whose friends belonged mostly to the *Mercure*. It was through Pound that Miss Barney gave a performance of George Antheil's music at her *salon*.

One day I went around to the rue Jacob to help Miss Barney look for one of my library books. She led me to a cupboard so stuffed with volumes that, when she opened the door, out fell one of them on the floor. It was Pound's *Instigations*. She said, "If you don't find your book, just take this instead." I protested that it was very rare, and pointed out that this copy was inscribed to her by the author, but she insisted on my taking it; she never read anything but poetry, kept nothing else in her library, she said.

At Miss Barney's one met the ladies with high collars and monocles, though Miss Barney herself was so feminine. Unfortunately, I missed the chance to make the acquaintance at her *salon* of the authoress of *The Well of Loneliness*, in which she concluded that if inverted couples could be united at the altar, all their problems would be solved.

It was at Miss Barney's that I saw Dolly Wilde, much resembling her Uncle Oscar but better looking. After her sad death in Venice, Miss Barney published a very touching tribute to her. Another of Miss Barney's friends whose life ended suddenly and, I believe, tragically was the poetess Renée Vivien.

Miss Barney, however, was not one to take a sad view of things. She was delightfully jolly, and the refreshments that she provided for her guests, particularly the chocolate cake from Colombin's, were of a very high order.

A little-known masterpiece by an anonymous author, probably Djuna Barnes, *The Lady's Almanach* is, so they say, a portrait of Miss Barney.

A lady who came to my bookshop with a letter from Miss Barney seemed to have got very little benefit from her visits to the rue Jacob. She looked overwrought, and hissed in my ear, "Have you anything more about *those unfortunate creatures?*"

THIRTEEN

Fitzgerald, Chamson, and Prévost

Adrienne was as interested as I was in the American writers who were in and out of my bookshop, and we shared them all. There should have been a tunnel under the rue de l'Odéon.

One of our great pals was Scott Fitzgerald—see the snapshot I took of him and Adrienne sitting on the doorstep of Shakespeare and Company. We liked him very much, as who didn't? With his blue eyes and good looks, his concern for others, that wild recklessness of his, and his fallen-angel fascination, he streaked across the rue de l'Odéon, dazzling us for a moment.

Scott worshiped James Joyce, but was afraid to approach him, so Adrienne cooked a nice dinner and invited the Joyces, the Fitzgeralds, and André Chamson and his wife, Lucie. Scott drew a picture in my copy of *The Great Gatsby* of the guests —with Joyce seated at the table wearing a halo, Scott kneeling beside him, and Adrienne and myself, at the head and foot, depicted as mermaids (or sirens).

Poor Scott was earning so much money from his books that he and Zelda had to drink a great deal of champagne in Montmartre in an effort to get rid of it. He spent an entire publisher's check on a pearl necklace for her. She made a present of the necklace to a Negress with whom she was dancing in one of the night clubs up there; but the girl returned it to her early next morning.

Scott and Zelda always left money on a plate in the hall of the house where they lived, so that people coming with bills

Paris, July 1928

18 Rue D'Odéon

Festival of St. James

or those to be tipped could simply help themselves. Thus did Scott shed all he earned without concern for the future.

It was through Scott, I imagine, that I met King Vidor, of Hollywood, and through me that Scott met the young French writer André Chamson.

This is the way I fell in and out with Hollywood. King Vidor came to the bookshop one day to ask me if I knew any young French author who might have a book he could use for a film. I thought immediately of André Chamson's first novel, *The Road*. This was an exciting, dramatic story, a true one, about the building of a road on Chamson's native mountain, l'Aigual, in the Cévennes. The village at the foot of the mountain that he described was the one where he had been born and raised. It was a striking and beautiful tale that this young Cevennol told, and one that Chamson himself had lived.

So I suggested *The Road* to King Vidor, telling him what the story was about. "Why, that's just what I'm looking for," he said, and, at Vidor's request, I asked Chamson to drop in at the bookshop.

Vidor came back, bringing Eleanor Boardman with him to work with Chamson on the scenario. He knew no French, and Chamson no English, but I interpreted for them and was delighted when the scenario seemed to be emerging. Vidor's reputation in Europe was then at its height, and he didn't disappoint me as a man: he had depth and understanding, and very fine sensibilities.

The work on *The Road* had gone on for about a month when one day Vidor's big car failed to bring him to the bookshop rendezvous. A hastily scribbled note informed me that he had suddenly been called back to the United States—that's all. And that was the last we heard of him.

Many a time since then, Chamson and I have laughed—though we didn't think it funny at the time—over Vidor's promises to make Chamson a rich man. He expected the young writer to drop whatever he was doing in France and accompany him to Hollywood—where Chamson was to earn fabulous sums of money. Luckily, Chamson comes from a rather wise old race, and not for a minute did he do what they call *"perdre le nord"*—that is, he didn't go out of his course. He asked Vidor: "But what am I to do about my job?" Chamson had a good job—at the Chamber of Deputies, he was secretary to a Minister of State—and had no intention of abandoning his post.

All the same, I lost face in this affair, and, what was worse, so did my country. As for Scott Fitzgerald, he was horrified.

But he was so friendly about it all that Chamson soon forgave us for letting him down.

The Chamsons told me about a midnight visit from Scott in their little apartment behind the Pantheon. Scott had brought a bottle of champagne in a bucket that he must have picked up in a night club somewhere. After sharing the champagne with his friends, Scott thought he would stretch out on the divan—spend the night—so Lucie got a rug to put over him. Then he changed his mind, and they had some difficulty preventing him from diving off their balcony on to the street—they were six flights up. Chamson succeeded at last in getting Scott down the stairs, step by step, and into a taxi. He also prevented him from presenting the driver with all the money in his pocket, which the driver himself was anxious to avoid. "*Ça ferait des histoires*" ("That would get me into trouble"), he said. And, besides, taxi drivers are always honest men.

Chamson's career has been so brilliant that he has no cause to regret not following any will-o'-the-wisp. He became the youngest curator ever appointed at the Palais de Versailles. At present he is Curator at the Petit Palais and two other national museums, and has been elected a member of the Académie Française.

In the middle of the twenties, Adrienne and I saw a good deal of both André Chamson and Jean Prévost, close friends who were utterly unlike each other. Chamson was steady, studious, versatile, levelheaded; Prévost was rather erratic, temperamental, moody. He was a grammarian and of a philosophic turn of mind; Chamson was an art connoisseur, a historian, and political-minded.

Prévost was assistant editor of Adrienne Monnier's review for a while, so he spent much of his time around our bookshops. His great friend was André Maurois, to whom he was devoted, and who looked after him, and he was always talking about Maurois.

Adrienne and Chamson had mountains in common. And each

had a pet mountain. Chamson's was the Aigual in the Cévennes. Adrienne's was Les Déserts, high above Chambéry and Aix-les-Bains, between the two peaks, the Revard and the Croix de Nivolet.

To verify Chamson's claims, we drove down to the Cévennes to have a look at his Aigual, and were obliged to admit that his devotion was justified. It is tall, wooded, and literally stream-lined, since streams flow down its sides. Below is the Valley of Happiness, Vallée du Bonheur. The road winding to the top of Chamson's mountain—see his novel *The Road*—is, I must say, an achievement. And when you reach the top story of the Aigual, you look away over the Cévennes mountains to the Mediterranean. Nevertheless, Adrienne thought Chamson's mountain, with all its beauties, a mere hummock compared to her tough native Alps of Savoy.

Prévost was extremely hardheaded: I don't mean in a busi-ness sense, but literally; his head was as hard as a rock. He used to prove this by banging it against an iron pipe in my bookshop. It made the pipe and me shudder but he never felt it himself. He was a boxer and said that punches in the head didn't bother him; he didn't feel them. You might as well have punched an iron bar as Prévost's head. That was how Heming-way broke his thumb in the fight I organized between the two champs. Prévost was stocky in build and very strong. He went in for sports, and played football on Sundays.

Prévost was a graduate of the Ecole Normale, and one day, as we sat in Adrienne's library, she, Prévost, and I, a man stopped to look at the books in the window—a middle-aged man, very interesting looking. Prévost said, "There's Herriot," and rushed out. He gave Herriot the Ecole Normale salutation (too obscene to quote), and Herriot followed him into the bookshop. I liked Eduard Herriot and admired him as one of the best of French statesmen. Besides, he always liked my country. I ran across the street to Shakespeare and Company to fetch my copy of *Amid the Forests of Normandy*, which he very kindly signed for me.

Prévost, who minded the slightest ailments, such as a cold or a pain in the stomach, was not afraid of death. He died in the Resistance.

A. MacLeish

Two of the American members of the Shakespeare and Company family of whom I was very fond were Ada and Archibald MacLeish. The author of *The Happy Marriage* and *The Pot of Earth* came to the bookshop in 1924, or was it later? I'm not sure of the year. Archie inscribed the first of these two little books to me in 1928, but he was an old friend by 1926. He was a friend of Joyce's too; both he and Ludwig Lewissohn worked on the wording of the protest against the pirating of *Ulysses*.

I remember MacLeish and Hemingway meeting at the bookshop to discuss a certain plan to rescue Hart Crane, who for some reason was in a predicament with the French police. This was the sort of thing that happened to some of our friends with too many drinks in them and too few French words. Luckily, they had MacLeish and Hemingway in these emergencies.

Adrienne and I dined at the MacLeishes' one evening, in their elegant little house, situated on that grand avenue du Bois de Boulogne which has now been renamed avenue Foch. The house and the lackey in white gloves had been lent to the MacLeishes by a friend, as they explained somewhat apologetically.

After supper, Archie read us a partly finished poem, and Ada sang—she had a beautiful voice. The Joyces were there. Joyce was very fond of Ada's singing, and he coached her in the Irish songs from his repertory before her concert, which we all attended.

Ballet Mécanique

Shakespeare and Company became involved at one time with music. After we moved to the rue de l'Odéon, George Antheil and Böske lived in the two-room apartment above the bookstore—which was just as well, because George had a big appetite for books and devoured every one of the volumes in my library. Customers looking at the pictures on the walls would invariably ask who that was in the photograph by Man Ray—that fellow with bangs. At that very moment, the side door of the library might open and the fellow himself come in, carrying an armful of books. George gave me a valuable suggestion for getting rid of my books. He offered to give all the volumes in the window more exciting titles. They would sell right off, he said, and when I heard some of the unmentionable titles he proposed, I thought it quite likely that they would.

If George had forgotten his key and Böske was out, he would climb up, with the help of the Shakespeare sign, and hoist himself through his window on the second floor. Passersby stopped to look; it was another of those Westerns provided by my customers. They whistled up and down the street, and some of them even dressed like cowboys. My concierge, an old lady with a medal for forty years of faithful service, liked Americans. She said, "We Americans," and thought we were almost as amusing as the races. In her preconcierge years, her husband had driven a coach to Longchamps, and it was she, with a leather bag strapped over her shoulder and hanging on as the coach swayed, who collected the fares. "That American," she used to say, referring to my dog, Teddy, who always wore his Brooklyn license. She was especially fond of George Antheil, except when he came home late at night and she had to let him in.

George's tastes and mine, as far as *Ulysses* was concerned, were similar. It "works," said George. He spoke of it as though it were a mechanical invention. He dreamed of composing an opera inspired by *Ulysses,* but, unfortunately, he never produced it.

Adrienne and I were in on the *Ballet Mécanique* from the beginning. Antheil had no piano at the time he was working on it, so she let him use the one in her apartment, since she was in her bookshop all day. The piano is a percussion instrument, and that was the impression you got when George played it, or, rather, punched it. A woman who swept Adrienne's rooms used to listen, leaning on her broom, to what she called "The Firemen." She found it curious but stirring.

We followed the progress of this composition with great excitement. And when it was finished, we were invited to hear it played by George on a player piano at Pleyel's. There were three rolls. Adrienne, Joyce, Robert McAlmon, myself, and some others were present, and, of course, Böske, who was needed to rub down the performer after his efforts—he was dripping.

Antheil said that the *Ballet Mécanique* was composed for a player piano because it was technically impossible for human hands to play it, but he had almost as much work as the piano. Every one of us, including Joyce, liked the *Ballet* very much, but Joyce regretted that "the pianistic contortions" had not been eliminated by the mechanical piano.

With the help of Bryher's mother, Lady Ellerman, Antheil was able to hold out until he finished the *Ballet.* Then Mrs. Bok sent him a check to cover the expenses of its performance. The immense Théâtre des Champs Elysées was hired, and Vladimir Golschmann, who took a great interest in Antheil's music, consented to conduct the *Ballet Mécanique* and his symphony, which was to come first on the program.

Meanwhile, "M. et Mme. Ezra Pound" sent us an invitation to a private concert to hear some of the compositions of Pound and Antheil. This concert of two musical conspirators was held at the Salle Pleyel, in one of the small rooms. Adrienne and I were seated with Joyce and his son, Georgio.

Joyce had brought Georgio along in the hope of converting him to modern music, but Pound's and Antheil's compositions were hardly the best choice for that purpose. Margaret Anderson and Jane Heap were present. So were Djuna Barnes and Ernest Hemingway.

The program was headed: "Musique Américaine: (Declaration of Independence): performed by Olga Rudge & George Antheil."

The performance of the *Ballet Mécanique* at the Théâtre des Champs Elysées in 1925 was one of the big events of the twenties. The entire "Crowd" turned up and packed the big theatre. When we arrived, though it was some time before the hour of the concert, the place was full, and out front was a struggling mob trying to get in. We had great difficulty reaching our seats; like the "mausoleum" of the Turk, it was "full inside." We looked around. There was plenty of time for that because George Antheil couldn't put on his tails until his friend Alan Tanner had darned the moth hole in the front, and the concert couldn't begin without the chief pianist. There were the Joyces in a box. There was our rarely seen T. S. Eliot, so handsome and so elegantly attired, and with him was Princess Bassiano. Up in the top gallery, the center of a group of Montparnassians, was Ezra Pound to see that George Antheil got a fair deal. In the orchestra, a distinguished-looking lady in black was bowing to everybody very graciously. Royalty, it was whispered. "It's your concierge," Adrienne exclaimed.

The audience was strangely affected by the *Ballet Mécanique*. The music was drowned out by yells from all over the house. Objectors on the floor were answered by defenders above; Ezra's voice was heard above the others', and someone said they saw him hanging head downward from the top gallery.

You saw people punching each other in the face, you heard the yelling, but you didn't hear a note of the *Ballet Mécanique*, which, judging by the motions of the performers, was going on all the time.

But these angry people suddenly subsided when the plane propellers called for in the score began whirring and raised a breeze that, Stuart Gilbert says, blew the wig off the head of a man next to him and whisked it all the way to the back of the house. Men turned up their coat collars, the women drew their wraps around them; it was quite chilly.

Well, one couldn't say that the *Ballet Mécanique* had had a hearing, but at least George Antheil had a *chahut* and, from a Dada point of view, one couldn't have anything better.

It seemed to me that George Antheil should now bury himself in his work. Others urged him to profit by all the publicity to get some more of it. Pound, George told me, suggested that he set out on a walking tour through Italy with his cat, Crazy, on his back. But George didn't like walking, particularly with Crazy on his back. As for Crazy, he preferred walking along the balcony to visit his feminine friends next door.

Finally, George Antheil disappeared into the African jungle "in search of rhythms"; he found a spot where the music was "nothing but sticks." Then no more was heard of him. I was sorry I had ever had a book called *African Swamps* in my library, and I was anxious about George. So was his father, who had seen the newspaper reports and sent me a cable asking if I had any news of his son. The telephone in my shop rang incessantly. I was beginning to feel very anxious when, happily, Antheil turned up.

A friend of George Antheil's and of mine was the brilliant young American writer and composer Virgil Thomson. He was also a friend of Gertrude Stein's. His compositions were performed at the various musical *salons* in Paris, particularly at the *salon* of the famous Madame Du Bost, where Stravinsky and "The Six"—and Antheil, too—were heard.

In 1928, an American in Paris dropped in at Shakespeare and Company to buy a copy of *Ulysses:* George Gershwin. A very attractive, lovable fellow was Gershwin. A lady I had never met gave a party for the Gershwins and invited me. You didn't have to shake hands with your hostess because nobody could point her out in the throng that kept pouring from the elevator into her apartment and shoving their way toward the grand piano at which George Gershwin was seated. His brother, Ira, and his sister, Frances, a very pretty girl, were standing by him, and his sister sang some of his songs. George, too, sang, and played his piano pieces.

FOURTEEN

The Silver Ship

By the middle twenties, French readers were extremely interested in American writers, and Adrienne Monnier had done much to develop this interest. In 1925, she published in *Le Navire d'Argent* the first French translation of "Prufrock." We translated it together; not very well, perhaps, but at least it was a work of love, and we never heard any reproaches from our victim. Then, in March, 1926, Adrienne published an all-American number of *Le Navire d'Argent*. It started off with a political speech by Walt Whitman entitled "The Eighteenth Presidency," which had been discovered by a young French professor named Jean Catel. Catel believed it to be an unpublished work of Whitman's, and perhaps it was. Adrienne and I translated this speech. The poet himself had printed it —in such small type that I came near blinding myself working on it. I went to Joyce's oculist. That same day, Joyce's birthday, I attended his birthday party, and behold! both Joyce and his publisher wearing a black bandage over one eye.

In Adrienne's all-American number, she published, in addition to the Whitman speech, the work of *"Quatre Jeunes Etats-Uniens"*—William Carlos Williams, Robert McAlmon, Ernest Hemingway, and E. E. Cummings. It was the first appearance in French of these writers. Included was an extract from Williams' *The Great American Novel* (*Le Grand Roman américain*), translated by Auguste Morel, the translator of *Ulysses*; Hemingway's story "The Undefeated" (*"Invincible"*); an extract from Cummings' *The Enormous Room* entitled "Sipliss," translated by George Duplaix; and a story by McAlmon, "The Publicity Agent," (*Agence de Publicité*), translated by Adrienne and myself.

This number also contained a part of Adrienne's *Bibliographie américaine*. She had undertaken the job, not an easy one, of compiling a catalogue of all the American writings that had been translated into French. She had already completed a similar bibliography of English literature. Strange to say, there had been no previous cataloguing of translations. She received no reward except personal satisfaction.

Whitman in Paris

It was at about this time, too, that I put on an exhibition in honor of Walt Whitman. Whitman was anything but the style. "The Crowd" couldn't put up with him, especially after T. S. Eliot aired *his* views about Walt. Only Joyce and the French and I were still old-fashioned enough to get along with Whitman. I could see with half an eye Whitman's influence on Joyce's work—hadn't he recited some lines to me one day?

Jo Davidson, when he heard I was about to put on a Walt Whitman exhibition, came to tell me about a plan that was under way to place a statue of Walt Whitman at the Battery in New York. There was to be an avenue of trees leading up to it, with benches on either side where people could linger at the lunch hour. Jo Davidson had been commissioned to do the statue—it was a sort of walking Walt to symbolize the open road—and wanted me to include a replica of the piece among my exhibits. I was delighted to hear that Manhattan was planning to honor Walt Whitman, and to contribute the gate receipts from my show to the fund that was being raised.

Jo Davidson brought me the replica of his statue—along with some interesting photographs of Walt; and I was able to borrow a lot of valuable early editions, some letters and other items—it was surprising to find how much material on Whitman was available in French collections. And of course Shakespeare and Company had its own permanent Whitman items, the little manuscripts my Aunt Agnes Orbison had saved from the wastebasket on her visit to Camden.

The exhibition was ready. All that was lacking was an American flag of suitable dimensions, which I needed to screen off the bookshelves—and to add a patriotic note. Walt Whitman always brings out my patriotism. And though flags, I think, should be the "Wild Flag" sort that E. B. White wrote about, I just happened to possess what was perhaps the largest American flag in Paris. I had got it marked down at the Louvre Magasins. It was a great-building-size flag, a leftover from World War I. It was very effective at Walt Whitman's exhibition.

Years later, I was to obtain possession of a second immense American flag, which I got right off a building—the National Cash Register building in Paris. This was during the Liberation. The Germans dropped a bomb on the building. The morning after this disaster, as I was coming out of Notre Dame Cathedral, which was in the vicinity of the building that had vanished, I met a man carrying two of the largest flags I have ever seen, one American and one French. On questioning the man—which, in view of the circumstances, was natural —I found that he was an employee of the National Cash Register Company and was taking the flags to a safe place. He immediately transferred his burden to my arms. I had to walk all the way home with them, but stranger things were to be seen in the Paris of the Liberation.

To get back to the Whitman exhibition, it was a great success, and in a *Ulysses*-sized morocco-bound book I have the signatures, headed by that of Paul Valéry, of the many visitors who came to see it.

Contact and Three Mountains

Shakespeare and Company was in close touch with the small presses in Paris that published books in English. A pioneer among them was Robert McAlmon's Contact Publishing Company; he announced his plans in the first number of F. M. Ford's *Transatlantic Review:*

At intervals of two weeks to six months, or six years, we will bring out books by various writers who seem not likely to be published by other publishers, for commercial or legislative reasons. . . . Three hundred only of each book will be printed. These books are published simply because they are written, and we like them well enough to get them out. Anybody interested may communicate with Contact Publishing Co., 12 rue de l'Odéon, Paris.

In New York, McAlmon and William Carlos Williams had collaborated in what they called the "Contact movement." They had published one or two numbers of the *Contact Review* when McAlmon migrated to Paris. I never quite understood what the "Contact movement" was about, but the books McAlmon published in Contact Editions were quite out of the ordinary. For instance, there was a small blue book called *Three Stories & Ten Poems* by a new writer named Ernest Hemingway. It sold out immediately, and made both Hemingway and Contact Editions famous. Then there was a collection of stories by McAlmon himself. The title, suggested by Joyce as characteristic of the author, was *A Hasty Bunch*. This was McAlmon's first book of prose, I think, though a volume of his poems, *Explorations*, had been published in England by the Egoist Press.

Contact brought out Bryher's *Two Selves* and H. D.'s *Palimpsest*. Another volume was a novel by Mary Butts, *Ashe of Rings*. Like everything else of hers, it is now very much sought after; one day, let us hope, there will be a complete edition of the work of Mary Butts. John Herrman contributed an amusing tale about a drummer entitled *What Happens. My First Twenty Years* by Gertrude Beasley, a Texas school-teacher, was anything but dull. And, of course, one of the first Contact books, *The Hurried Man*, was by a poet "the Crowd" looked after, Emanuel Carnevali, who was lying ill in Milan. Other Contact titles were Ken Sato's *Quaint Stories, Twenty-Five Poems* by Marsden Hartley, *Spring and*

Signatures of authors,
CONTACT COLLECTION OF
CONTEMPORARY WRITERS

all by William Carlos Williams, Mina Loy's *Lunar Baedecker* (which I understand is about to be reissued in the United States), *Sailors Don't Care* by Edwin Lanham, *Eater of Darkness* by Robert Coates, and two more volumes of short stories by McAlmon, *A Companion Volume* and *Post Adolescence*—this last was my favorite work of his. Finally, there was an anthology, the *Contact Collection of Contemporary Writers*, which was made up of extracts of whatever the writers happened to be working on at the time. It was the most interesting book of scraps I ever saw. It contained the first published piece

of *Finnegans Wake,* with the title "From 'Work in Progress,' "
and contributions from all the writers worth mentioning of that
period.

Manuscripts for Contact Editions were submitted to Mc-
Almon at the Dôme Café, and he told me he discovered most
of his writers at one café or another.

McAlmon's friend and fellow-publisher was William Bird.
Bill Bird was a prominent member of the press in Paris, who
spent his spare money and time on the little, entirely personal,
editions of the Three Mountains Press. He had heard from a
fellow-writer of a bargain hand press that was available, and
installed it in a tiny office on the Ile Saint Louis. He was engaged in printing a book when I went to see him one day.
He had to come out onto the sidewalk to see me because, as
he explained, in his "office" there was room only for the
hand press and the printer-editor. Bill Bird knew all about rare
editions. He was a bibliophile, and his publications were everything a collector could wish—they were printed in handsome
type on large pages of fine paper, and the editions were
limited. Bird brought out Pound's *Cantos* and *Indiscretions,*
Ernest Hemingway's *In Our Time,* and F. M. Ford's *Women
and Men,* among others. Bill was a great connoisseur of wines,
too; the only one of his publications that was not on large
paper was a booklet called *French Wines.* The author was
William Bird.

Jack Kahane

Another friend and colleague in the publishing business was
Mr. Jack Kahane, a gassed war veteran from Manchester,
England. I liked him for his good humor and scorn of pretenses.
The Vendôme Press and the Obelisk Press belonged to him, and
very little of his time and money was wasted on anything but

the spicy kind of books. He himself contributed to the supply
of these in a series by "Cecil Barr" that he called "my Flowers"
with titles such as *The Daffodil*. Besides the "Flowers," he was
the author of *The Browsing Goat*. Kahane was married to a
Frenchwoman, and they had a large family of children to bring
up on the "Flowers."

Mr. Kahane used to drive up in his convertible Voisin,
a sort of glass-enclosed station wagon, for a chat with his colleague at Shakespeare and Company. He would ask, "How's
God?" (meaning Joyce). He admired me "no end" for my
discovery of such an "obscene" book, as he termed it, as
Ulysses, and never relinquished the hope of persuading me one
day to let the Obelisk Press take it over. Meanwhile, he was
obliged to be content with an extract from Joyce's new work,
entitled *Haveth Childers Everywhere*, which Kahane thought
lacking in sex interest. Kahane and his partner, M. Babou,
brought out a very fine edition of *H.C.E.* and, some time later,
of *Pomes Penyeach* with Joyce's daughter Lucia's lettering and
decorations of the text. They remind one of *The Book of Kells*,
a favorite of her father's. You can see its influence on the
lettering of *Pomes*. Joyce was delighted when he found I
possessed *The Book of Kells*. It was the only ancient illumi-
nated book that was humorous, according to him.

The Crosbys

Harry and Caresse Crosby wanted a piece of "Work in Progress," and I went around to see them one day about "Two
Tales of Shem and Shaun." Their Black Sun Press was in a
little old street, the rue Cardinale, a few steps from Saint
Germain des Prés. The Crosbys were among the most charming people I ever knew. They were connoisseurs of fine books,
but, better still, of fine writing. They brought out Hart Crane's
The Bridge and Archibald MacLeish's *Einstein*, among others.
One of their publications that few people seem to have noticed

was Henry James's *Letters to Walter Berry*, interesting and pathetic communications from a Henry James nearing the end of his life, trying to fend off the gift of a fine suitcase that he would never use. Harry Crosby was, I believe, a nephew, or maybe a cousin, of Walter Berry, himself an interesting character.

The Crosby volume was entitled *Tales Told of Shem and Shaun*, and contained my favorite "Mookes and the Gripes" and "The Ondt and the Gracehoper," which I think are certainly the most extraordinary linguistic feats ever performed by this prodigious master of words, not to mention their peculiar poetic charm.

This Mookes fellow was Joyce's good-humored retort to the attacks of *The Enemy*, Wyndham Lewis's review. It is an example of Joyce's gentle way of retaliating when attacked, one of those playful little inventions, almost whispered, half concealed in the strange Joycean atmosphere—and quite harmless, almost affectionate.

A third "Tale" might be told, that of the portrait of Joyce that Brancusi was asked by the Crosbys to draw as a frontispiece for the book. Joyce sat for his portrait. It resembled the sitter but disappointed the publishers. Brancusi tried again, and drew something that he said was Joyce reduced to the essentials; this time it was a success—a real Brancusi!

I was so old-fashioned as to prefer the portrait that resembled Joyce, and Brancusi, who was laughing over the story with Katherine Dudley not long ago, told her he wanted to have the pleasure of making me a present of the original drawing. The one in "Two Tales" is, I fear, too essential for me.

In his spare time, Harry Crosby was learning to pilot a plane: he was obsessed with death, and thought death by plane might be as good a one as any. He was fond of the Egyptian *Book of the Dead*, and presented Joyce with a fine copy of it—copies, rather, as it was in three volumes. He was a nervous chap, too nervous, I thought, to pilot a plane, even if that sort of death did appeal to him. He used to dart in and out of my bookshop, dive into the bookshelves like a humming-bird extracting honey from a blossom, or hover a minute around my table to tell me that it was he who had told his wife one day that her name was Caresse, and had gone hand

*Brancusi's portrait
of James Joyce*

in hand with her to the *mairie* to have it legalized. He brought me one day snapshots of them both in front of his plane—the day he got his pilot's license. He didn't often show me his poetry—a proof of his modesty. He had a light touch in every-thing, much charm, and a great deal of kindness.

He was generous in his dealings with Joyce, that is to say, with me for Joyce. It was my business, of course, to arrange everything with the publishers of these pieces from "Work in Progress" and to get as much as I could for them. I was very grasping in matters concerning Joyce, and was reputed to be hardheaded in business. Nobody around us, however, had the slightest illusion on the subject. Shakespeare and Company was given power of attorney by Joyce to deal with his affairs, but no profit was derived from it—services were free. The publishers, aware of this, always presented me with a specially fine copy of their book, and Joyce always inscribed it "with gratitude."

Plain Edition

Several years prior to World War II, Getrude Stein and Alice B. Toklas did some publishing under the imprint of Plain Edition, at their own address, 27 rue de Fleurus. They brought out several of Gertrude's books, including one of my favorites, *Lucy Church Amiably*, and a volume entitled *Operas and Plays* that contained the famous *Four Saints in Three Acts*. When this play, with music by Virgil Thomson (a former customer of Shakespeare and Company), was performed in New York, the book was in such demand that it sold out immediately. The Plain Edition volumes were attractively produced and very popular with my Stein fans. The print and paper were nice, and the little volumes reminded me of our pioneer of the twenties, the Contact Editions of Robert McAlmon.

About the last of the little American publishing houses in Paris was Miss Barbara Harrison's Harrison Press. With the help of an expert, Monroe Wheeler, Miss Harrison brought out some fine editions. Among them were Katherine Anne Porter's *Hacienda* and her *French Song Book*, which must be very rare items now.

Gargoyle and *Transatlantic*

The best way of following the literary movement in the twenties is through the little reviews, often short-lived, alas! but always interesting. Shakespeare and Company never published one. We had enough to do taking care of those published by our friends.

The first one, I think, was Arthur Moss's *Gargoyle*. Florence Gilliam was its coeditor. *Gargoyle* had a "*chimère*" on the cover, but, as a French architect pointed out to me, it was a very different animal from a gargoyle. The French don't like the identity of their pets to be confused. *Gargoyle* ran to very few, but interesting, numbers.

Then there was the *Transatlantic Review*. Ford Madox Hueffer, former editor of the exciting *English Review*, had been enticed to come to Paris. He left the "Hueffer" part of him behind, and was known from then on as Ford Madox Ford. He had been gassed in the war, but it had not affected his activities. He was a jolly creature, and popular with his fellow writers: he had the reputation of reaching down into his own pocket to pay contributors to the *English Review* when other funds were not available.

Ford used a ship as the device for the *Transatlantic* and also part of the Paris motto, "*Fluctuat*"—but he prudently left out the "*nec Mergitur.*"

The first thing he and his wife, Stella Bowen, did was to invite "the Crowd" to a party in the big studio that had been lent to them. There was dancing to an accordion and plenty of beer and cheese and other refreshments. Ford invited me to dance with him, first making me take off my shoes—he was already in his bare feet. With Ford, it was more bouncing and prancing than dancing. I saw Joyce watching us from the sidelines with great amusement.

On another occasion, Ford and Stella invited me to supper.

By that time they were installed in a smaller studio with a
soupente, where the table was spread. Ford himself cooked
the meal of fried eggs and bacon, and very nicely, too. After
supper, Ford paced up and down reading aloud to me a poem
he had just finished. It was about Heaven and was quite interesting, at least what I heard of it. I hope Ford didn't notice
that I kept falling asleep. I had to get up so early in the morning that if a poem of any length was read to me in the evening
it put me to sleep at once. This was unfortunate, for he may
have been reading me his new poem with the hope that Shakespeare and Company would publish it, though he never went
so far as to suggest it to me. I'm afraid some of the writers
didn't like my exclusiveness in publishing only Joyce, but
perhaps they didn't realize that I was almost swamped already
with my one author.

In the first number of *Transatlantic Review*, Ford published
a most amusing letter from T. S. Eliot. Joyce's "Four Old
Men" appeared in No. 4. Shortly, funds began to run low,
as I remember, and the editor crossed the Atlantic to try to
raise money to keep his ship afloat. He left Hemingway in
command during his absence, and the review was quite lively
by the time Ford returned.

In spite of its interesting editor and contributors, the *Transatlantic Review* went down. It was much missed by its readers
and by the many writers whose manuscripts were available
abroad in those years.

Ernest Walsh and *This Quarter*

One day a note was brought me from Claridge's, from a young
man named Ernest Walsh. Enclosed was a letter of introduction from someone in Chicago. Walsh apologized for not
coming himself. He was too ill to leave his bed. He told me
his situation. His funds had given out and unless he could get
help, he would have to move away from Claridge's.

I wondered what Shakespeare and Company was expected to do in the circumstances, and was too busy to leave the bookshop, but I sent a friend in my place to see what could be done for Walsh. The friend found the poet lying in bed in one of the best suites in the hotel. He had indeed been very ill, and under the care of a doctor and day and night nurses, and was still too sick to be moved.

My friend found out that Walsh had arrived in the company of two delightful young persons whom he had met on the boat. His illness was due to a cold he had caught driving with them in the Bois de Boulogne. The girls had disappeared, probably to look for someone with plenty of money. Walsh had spent all he had. My friend noticed the gold-stoppered whisky bottle on the table, the magnificent dressing gown thrown over a chair, and the fine clothes in the open wardrobe.

The management at Claridge's had been kind, but they were beginning to insist. Their guest couldn't stay if he couldn't pay, and they even talked of getting in touch with the Embassy.

Luckily for Walsh, he had a letter to Mr. Pound also, and Ezra, who made a business of rescuing poets, hurried round. Presently I heard that the poet's financial problems had been solved, and I saw that he had recovered from his illness when he appeared at the bookshop with a woman who had befriended him. His benefactress was Miss Ethel Moorhead, a Scotch poetess, formerly a militant suffragette who had blown up pillar boxes. Ernest Walsh was her next most explosive adventure. The two of them, by this time, had decided to start a review to be called *This Quarter*, and they planned to publish it on the Riviera, since the climate in Paris didn't suit Walsh.

I liked the two of them very much, and I admired their courage and their passion for poetry. They carried out their plans, and brought out several lively numbers. The first one was dedicated to Ezra Pound's work. No. 2 contained the piece about "Shem" from Joyce's "Work in Progress," and contributions from many other writers who were about in that exciting "Paris period" of America's literary history.

Later Kay Boyle assisted Ernest Walsh in editing his review. With her talent for writing and for motherhood, she is considered one of the interesting characters in the story of the twenties. When I first knew her, she was producing her early novels, *Plagued by the Nightingale*, which is built around her first marriage, and *Year Before Last*.

Ernest Walsh, as we learned later, knew that he had only a few months to live and he had decided to come to Paris to spend the time remaining to him among the writers he admired. He dreamed of making a name for himself as a poet, which was more difficult. There was something very fine about Ernest Walsh; he was alive and he was heroic.

transition

An important event in our literary life in Paris in the twenties was the appearance of the review *transition*.

A great friend of ours, Eugene Jolas, a young Franco-American writer who was very much "up" on the modern literary movement, came to tell me that he was leaving the staff of the Paris *Herald Tribune* to publish a review—in English, of course, and in Paris.

This was very good news. Reviews had come and gone, and it was just the right moment to launch a new one, particularly with such a competent editor as Jolas. I had a great liking not only for him personally, but also for his ideas.

Jolas asked me if I knew anything special he might use as a contribution to his review. It occurred to me that Joyce, instead of continuing to contribute bits of "Work in Progress" to reviews here and there, should publish it in monthly instalments in *transition*, if the editor approved. Jolas, and Elliot Paul, who was to assist him, received the suggestion with enthusiasm. Jolas immediately proposed to Joyce that he bring out the entire work in *transition*, and when Joyce called me up to ask what I thought of the plan, I advised him to accept without hesitation. I knew Jolas would be a friend he could depend on; and the name of James Joyce would be a great help in launching a new review.

Certainly one of the best things in Joyce's life was the friendship and collaboration of Maria and Eugene Jolas. From the time they first undertook to publish his work until his death, they rendered him every service and thought no sacrifice too great.

Eugene Jolas, with his three mother tongues, English, French, and German (he was from Lorraine), and James Joyce, the multilinguist, set out to revolutionize the English language. They had plenty of words at their disposal and they didn't see what could prevent them from getting all the fun in the world out of them. The reinforcement brought by Jolas was a godsend to Joyce, who was feeling rather lonely with his one-man revolution till *transition* came along.

Jolas was for a democracy of letters, an idea I didn't always agree with. He told me he never refused the manuscript of an unknown writer. That was a principle with him, and I saw it had its advantages. At least newcomers weren't frozen out. If you look over the files of *transition*, you will see how extraordinary was its scope. All the best Anglo-Saxon and European work of the period appeared in it, much of it for the first time. Of all the reviews I came in contact with, *transition* was the most vital, the longest-lived, and the review that I felt was most intelligently devoted to the interests of new writing.

After Elliot Paul's departure, the first collaborator of Eugene Jolas was Robert Sage; others connected with *transition* were Matthew Josephson, Harry Crosby, Carl Einstein, Stuart Gilbert, and James Johnson Sweeney.

Commerce

Only the English-language reviews of the twenties in Paris come into my story, with the exception of *Commerce*, for *Commerce*, though its contributions were in French, belonged to an American, the Princess Bassiano, or, as she prefers to be called, Marguerite Caetani.

Commerce appeared first in 1924; our friends were contributors, and it was published by Adrienne Monnier at her bookshop in the rue de l'Odéon. Paul Valéry was its editor, assisted by Valery Larbaud and Léon-Paul Fargue. Saint-John Perse was a contributor, and his presence was indicated by the title, which was suggested by a line from *Anabase:* "*ce pur commerce de mon âme*" ("this pure commerce of my soul"). See T. S. Eliot's translation of this beautiful poem.

Marguerite Caetani was much admired by her French writer friends for her taste, intelligence, tact, and benevolence. They were quite jealous of Rome when it snatched her from Paris.

Adrienne Monnier was responsible for the production of *Commerce* and also for the extraction of contributions from Léon-Paul Fargue, which entailed the most exhausting labor. Fargue's ideas outran his lazy pen; he talked what he might have written. And working it up into something to appear in *Commerce* was poor Adrienne's job.

Fargue, by the way, was such a brilliant talker that he was much in demand by hostesses; but he was a trial to them, too. I think of the time Marguerite Caetani invited her *Commerce* friends to lunch at her house in Versailles. She sent a car to fetch us. The chauffeur called first for Adrienne and me in the rue de l'Odéon. We picked up Joyce at the Square Robiac, and then went over to the Gare de l'Est region to the abode of Léon-Paul Fargue. The chauffeur went upstairs to tell him that we were waiting below. He was not up yet: he was writing a cat poem, his cats around him on his bed. He would get up and dress and come right down. We waited more than an hour. He finally came down, but he went right up again because he had decided that black shoes would look better with his suit than the brown ones he was wearing; and then, a second time, to change his hat. Before getting into the car, he asked the chauffeur to look around for a barbershop; he needed a shave and a haircut. It was Sunday, and of course all the barbershops were closed. We did find one at last. The barber was just closing this one, but he was persuaded by Fargue to give him a shave and a haircut, and they disappeared inside. After that was done, there was nothing to prevent our going to lunch at Versailles, and off we went.

Adrienne was worried about our being late. Fargue had no watch. He consulted Joyce, who was wearing four, all telling a different time of day. The lunch was supposed to be at one. For a wonder, we were only an hour and a half late. Not a word of reproach from Marguerite Caetani. She was quite unruffled, and laughing as usual. As for the guests, they were used to waiting for Fargue.

At this lunch, celebrating *Commerce* and the appearance in No. 1 of the first extract from the French translation of *Ulysses*, Joyce's presence was counted on. He never accepted middle-of-the-day invitations; not till the evening did he feel ready to be sociable. But I persuaded him to come this time. I thought he wouldn't regret it; he did, for we had hardly sat down at table when a large, shaggy dog trotted in, made straight for Joyce, and, putting his big paws on his shoulders, looked lovingly into his face.

Poor Joyce! As soon as the Princess Bassiano realized his case, she had man's best friend removed, telling Joyce at the same time that the animal was harmless, the children's pet. Once, to be sure, it had chased a plumber out the window. "I had to buy the man a new pair of trousers," she said, laughing.

Joyce shuddered and whispered to me, "She's going to have to do the same thing for me."

Our Friend Stuart Gilbert

The extract in *Commerce* from the French translation of *Ulysses* attracted the attention of a great authority on the subject of this work. Soon after its publication in *Commerce*, I had a visit from Stuart Gilbert, or simply Gilbert, since that is the French way.

I always enjoyed the visits of this delightfully humorous, witty, paradoxical, rather cynical, extremely kind Englishman. He had been a judge in Burma for nine years, and, according to him, his job was hanging people. But I think that story should be sifted. It doesn't fit our Gilbert at all; he has too many deeds of kindness to answer for to get away with that.

Gilbert was one of the first admirers of *Ulysses*, and had brought his considerable learning to bear on it. I don't think anybody, except perhaps Joyce, knew as much about this work as he did. His sharp eye had perceived one or two errors in the extract of the French version that had just appeared in *Commerce*, slips that might occur even when the translator was as competent as Auguste Morel, the young poet who had undertaken this immense task. Adrienne Monnier and Larbaud admired Morel's translations of Francis Thompson, Blake, Donne, and others, and, under their persuasion, he interrupted a whole anthology of English poets to take up the work on *Ulysses*. He made one condition, that Larbaud should revise his translation. Now it was finished—this was in 1924—and they were then going over it together. Stuart Gilbert had come to suggest that if Larbaud and Morel would accept his services, an Englishman's help might be useful.

Gilbert's proposal was immediately accepted by Adrienne Monnier, who was to publish the translation of *Ulysses*, and by Larbaud and Morel. His help was indeed indispensable in such a difficult enterprise as theirs. Thanks to Gilbert, certain mistakes were avoided and obscurities removed, and I am sure he rendered a great service to the translator and also to Larbaud, who was to be responsible for the translation.

The collaborators had their troubles, of course, and in the *mic-macs* Adrienne was the principal sufferer. Because Larbaud not only revised, but rewrote, an occasional line, Morel objected. He had a temper and said things, I believe, to Larbaud. Then he got annoyed at Gilbert, who, he thought, was too exacting, and went away in a huff. Meanwhile, Larbaud, whose health was never good, fell ill and retired to his home near Vichy. The survivors, Gilbert and Adrienne, spent many an afternoon, so he tells me, completing the work in the back room of her bookshop.

FIFTEEN

Jules Romains and the "Copains"

I first read Jules Romains in the translation by Desmond Mac-Carthy and Sydney Waterlow of *La Mort de Quelqu'un* (*Death of a Nobody*), which I discovered in the New York Public Library around 1914. It fascinated me, and, after this initiation into the world of Jules Romains, I followed his work closely. Though quite different in many ways, Jules Romains and James Joyce have much, I think, in common: more than with any of their contemporaries.

Jules Romains, who came frequently to Adrienne's book-shop, used to make friendly visits to mine, and he very kindly included me as well as Adrienne whenever the "Copains," the characters in his book of stories of that name, held one of their reunions. These pals of Romains were delightful—a professor, his wife, who was also a professor, a painter, and the business manager of Jouvet's theatre. All were very amusing people; but Romains himself, the head conspirator—with Romains it was always a plot—was the ringleader.

We took turns entertaining each other, and often it was Romains and his wife who invited us to their house. At one time they occupied a villa up in Montmartre, or, rather, in Ménilmontant, a quarter that held many associations for Jules Romains. The street they lived in was rather isolated, and the neighborhood was notorious for Apaches, as gangsters were then called. Romains had installed a fierce mastiff to guard the villa. Even Romains' guests were afraid of him, and no Apache would have dared to approach the animal. All the same, as we sat there and the hour grew late, we listened for footsteps, and once we heard distinctly, first the sound of fumbling at a window on the floor below, and then a creaking. I hoped that if the Apaches turned up, they and the dog would settle their business down in the basement without bringing us into it.

Jules Romains took the "Copains" to the fascinating region of the canals, the scene of some of his stories. Few Parisians frequent these Dutch-looking quais, La Villette and the Canal St. Martin, or even know of their existence. I have often been back there since then.

Once, the "Copains" were invited to a rendezvous at a certain bistrot near "God Alley" (Passage Dieu). We were told to look as tough as we could, because it was that kind of a quarter. When Adrienne and I had managed to find the bistrot, we recognized some of the "Copains" in the fellows drinking red wine on the "zinc," or counter. Romains was nowhere to be seen, and we began to think that he wasn't going to turn up. Meanwhile, we noticed a character with a cap over one eye lounging at the corner outside and eying us in a not very reassuring way. Somebody did suggest that maybe that was Romains, but only as a joke. The fellow came into the bistrot; he was indeed Romains. He had managed a complete disguise.

A French Shakespearean

Georges Duhamel made many a friendly visit to Shakespeare and Company, whose name seemed to attract this French Shakespearean. Not only did he manifest his friendship for the bookshop, but he and Madame Duhamel invited its proprietor with Adrienne Monnier to spend a day at Valmondois, near Paris, where they had a house. Adrienne was one of Duhamel's publishers. Madame Duhamel, or Blanche Albane, as she was known in the theatre, was a member of Jacques Copeau's Vieux Colombier group and one of his most gifted actresses. She had an exceptional charm and grace, and I always loved hearing her at poetry recitals: verses recited by actors, even the greatest, sometimes leave a disappointing impression.

It was a summer day at Valmondois, and we much enjoyed watching Duhamel giving his first-born son, Bernard, a bath in a tub in the garden.

Jean Schlumberger

A friend for whom Adrienne and I had a great deal of admiration and affection was the author of *Un Homme Heureux*, Jean Schlumberger. The first trip we took in the Citroën we purchased on the instalment plan in 1927 was to Schlumberger's place in Normandy. He had invited us to spend the weekend, and I had promised to look over the family library of English novels and to throw out any of them that were not worth keeping.

This country house of Schlumberger's was built by his great-grandfather, the statesman and historian Guizot; and Braffye, as it is called, is a beautiful place. Schlumberger was brought up on it. So were his children, and he was very much attached to it. He preferred, however, to live and work, not in the big house, but in a cottage adjoining it. And it was here that we stayed with him and his two companions, a man and his wife who looked after him and cooked our delicious meals. There was a third companion, the dachshund, who, at her master's bidding, stood up on her hind legs to show us "the buttons on her waistcoat." It was very pleasant sitting with Schlumberger and dachshund in front of the fire that burned brightly with wood from his own trees.

Just as Schlumberger feared, the English library in the big house reflected the tastes of English governesses who had taught successive generations of young girls at Braffye.

Léon-Paul Fargue

The poet Léon-Paul Fargue, though he spoke not a word of English, haunted my bookshop. Fargue, one of the most interesting characters in the French literary world, was almost as good a word inventor as Joyce—he was a word maniac— but some of his richest creations were lost to those of his readers who had not been among his hearers. Adrienne's library was Fargue's headquarters. There you would see him any afternoon, and hear him telling the most awful stories to a circle of delighted listeners, "*les Potassons*," as he called his friends, among whom I had the honor to be counted. His verbal inventions were unimaginably obscene, and so were the gestures that accompanied them. And all this in a library where nice mothers of families and their *jeunes filles* were choosing books from the shelves. Larbaud was one of his most appreciative listeners. He would blush, chuckle, and say, "Oh!" in his Larbaldian manner. On the other hand Fargue's poems, in the rare volumes that appeared now and again, were chaste.

Fargue came to my bookshop, not for the books, but because of the possibility of finding some of his "*Potassons*" who might have escaped him elsewhere. It was a positive necessity for him to follow his friends everywhere. Once, when Larbaud didn't open his door, Fargue got a ladder and climbed up to the window. Larbaud told me he suddenly saw Fargue peering in at him as he sat working at his desk. A noctambule, Fargue rose toward the afternoon and, like a postman, started on his rounds.

Fargue always turned up sooner or later at Adrienne's bookshop; and it was there, or at Gallimard's, where he went on later, that all his friends, old and new, congregated. He was one of the founders of the *Nouvelle Revue Française* and an old school friend of Gaston Gallimard, its publisher. Fargue lingered in Adrienne's bookshop long after everyone else had departed, pouring out his many sorrows, while Adrienne was trying to close up.

He lived with his widowed mother and a long-suffering family servant at the glass factory that had been left to him by his father, an engineer, who had invented certain formulas in glassmaking. The factory was in the vicinity of the Gare de l'Est. Fargue said the whistling of the trains inspired him. He revered his father and was loath to part with the factory, which Fargue *père* had built up and which, under the proprietorship of a poet, was fast running down. The Fargue glass was well known in the days when *art nouveau* was flourishing. It decorated the houses of millionaires in the form of stained-glass windows and vases, all in the taste of the period. Fargue himself showed me a window at Maxim's that his father had done. The foreman, who had been there in the father's time, and who knew all the secret formulas, kept the place going, and every once in a while orders did come in. Then two extra workmen were called in to assist.

I visited the factory one day with Adrienne's sister Marie Monnier, who had been making some designs for Fargue's glass. They were busy turning out a lot of ceiling lights, sort of inverted soup plates decorated with weird figures from the Zodiac. The colors prevented any light from coming through, but maybe that was the intention. This sudden production was a scheme of Fargue's to revive the business, which at the time was fast flickering out. He was so sorrowful over its threatened extinction, a sad thing when you thought of his father, and the faithful foreman. We all hoped it might be prevented. I thought a little publicity might be timely, and I asked some New York *Times* people who were photographing the bookshop if they would do some pictures of Fargue at his factory. I have the photographs of Fargue at his factory showing a piece of his glasswork to a group of us, including the foreman and Julienne the maid.

As soon as a few specimens of the ceiling lights were ready, Fargue bundled them into a taxi and made the rounds of the department stores, and he talked the heads of many of the lighting-fixtures departments into giving him large orders. I imagine these people who knew the father's glass, and the son's poems, were quite amused by Fargue's visits.

Fargue was very much in demand socially, but he was a terrible trial to his hostesses, since he had not the slightest notion of time and was invariably late. They always forgave him, for when he did get there he entertained the company so wonderfully; and even while they waited for him, everybody had some story to tell of Fargue's doings—there were endless stories about him. That one, however, about his arriving two weeks late for dinner was enough to make any hostess shudder.

He always went around in taxis, which he kept waiting for hours, till finally the chauffeur would go looking for him. One of them once saw Fargue come out at last—and hail another taxi; he had entirely forgotten the one that had been waiting so long in front of the house.

A good many of these drivers seemed to be Fargue's personal friends, which explains their forbearance with his ways. One of them, who was introduced to me by Fargue as he was getting out of a taxi, was a reader of his poems and possessed rare editions of them, inscribed by the author.

Fargue was always introducing some new friend of his, someone with a fabulous fortune in Swiss cheeses, or that Spanish grandee he went around with for a while, or the cloth manufacturer with the striking name, Gabriel Latombe. And there was Gili Gili, the Egyptian magician, a very entertaining man who said, "Gili Gili" as he performed some sleight of hand.

Raymonde

One of my most interesting French friends was Raymonde Linossier, who, as I have already related, came to the rescue of the Circe episode when we were getting *Ulysses* into type. Soon after that, Joyce said, "I've put Raymonde into *Ulysses*."

Raymonde was the carefully brought-up daughter of a famous physician. She was supposed to be pursuing her studies at the neighboring law school, but if her father had not been too busy to watch her goings and comings, he might have discovered her almost any afternoon either at No. 7, where she was a prominent member of Adrienne Monnier's literary family and admitted as an authentic "*Potasson*" of the poet Léon-Paul Fargue's or at Shakespeare and Company, assisting, encouraging, and even at times replacing its proprietress.

It was difficult for an American girl like myself who had always been free to do what I pleased to understand the necessity for Raymonde's secretiveness. I couldn't make out at all why a young woman who mixed with the company at the Law Courts, who once even defended a prostitute, and had, in fact, made a considerable study of prostitution, must not be found in the vicinity of a Fargue or a Joyce.

Raymonde's best friend was Francis Poulenc. She had grown up with him, and their tastes and their ways of seeing things were identical. She divided her time between her poets in the rue de l'Odéon and her musical friends in the group known as "The Six." Darius and Madeleine Milhaud were her particular friends. They were my friends, too, especially Madeleine, who read all the new American books.

Raymonde was not a customer of mine. Her very restricted pocket money was reserved for French books. Fargue was her favorite poet, and she possessed everything he wrote, including most of his manuscripts. But she followed closely all my activities and took at least as much interest in them as in the

French goings-on at Adrienne's bookshop. She was herself a writer, and, of course, her writing, too, was clandestine. She was the author of a book entitled *Bibi-la-Bibiste*. According to the title page, it was written by "the X Sisters," Raymonde and her sister Alice, the present Dr. Alice Linossier-Ardoin. But Raymonde was actually the author—her sister had contributed her pocket money to the printing. They were very devoted to each other.

Bibi-la-Bibiste, which, translated, means practically "One's Self the One's Selfist," was dedicated to Francis Poulenc. It was printed on large paper, and its fourteen pages, including the title page, contain hardly any text at all. This "work" was quite a literary event in 1918, when I first met Raymonde. Ezra Pound seized upon it and sent it to the *Little Review*. It was printed in the issue of September-December 1920, with a note by "E. P." proclaiming it a chef-d'œuvre. It had, he said, "all the virtues required by the academicians: absolute clarity, absolute form, beginning, middle, and end." I don't think the French, nor particularly Raymonde herself, would have gone so far. Raymonde claimed to have founded a new movement, the "Selfist Movement"—it reminds me of what Valéry told me of his intention to found a "Self-Godding" Society, and, of course, we also had the *Egoist* in England. But Raymonde was far too modest and too humorous to be serious about *Bibi-la-Bibiste*. Those of us who knew her felt that she had the gift and the temperament of a writer, if only she had had a little more of the "Selfist" in her! A very great unselfishness and warm heart were, like her writing, clandestine, camouflaged by paradox and the comical. Specimens of this type do exist but are rare, particularly where there is talent.

A great musical friend of Raymonde's, and of mine, was Satie. Satie, perhaps because of English blood on one side of his family, seemed to like Shakespeare and Company. He called me "Mees," the only English word he knew, I imagine, and turned up regularly, always carrying an umbrella, rain or shine; no one had ever seen him without one. It was probably a wise precaution for somebody who came on a trolley from distant suburbs of Paris intending to stay in town all day.

Seeing me writing something, Satie asked me if I wrote. I said yes, business letters. He said that was the best kind of writing: good business writing had a definite meaning; you had something to say and you said it. That was the way I wrote, I told him.

Satie and Adrienne were good friends. His *Socrate* was heard for the first time at her bookshop. Fargue and Satie were cronies, then had a terrible falling out, I believe over an unfortunate incident in society circles where the composer and the poet shared popularity. At a certain *salon*, the master of ceremonies announced songs by Erik Satie but quite forgot to mention that the poems he had set to music were by Fargue. It was no doubt unintentional, and certainly it was not the fault of Satie, but Fargue was furious. As usual, in Fargue's feuds, he spent a good deal of time and took a lot of trouble to write the most dreadfully insulting things he could think of in daily letters to Satie. Not satisfied with mailing them in Paris, he would go all the way to Arcueil-Cachan, where Satie lived, to slip another insulting note under his door. Even the final one, too outrageous to repeat, failed to get anything but a laugh from Satie, a mild, philosophical-minded man, the composer, after all, of *Socrate*; and I think that was the last shot fired.

Eventually, Raymonde took up orientalism, which had always interested her, and after she was installed in an office of her own at the Guimet Museum, the orientalist museum in Paris, we saw her less frequently.

Raymonde lived with her sister until Alice married Dr. Ardoin. Raymonde then discovered a little apartment on the Quai Saint Michel, exactly the kind of place she liked. It had little low-ceilinged rooms, with bookcases filled with her rare editions and the manuscripts of Léon-Paul Fargue, her favorite poet.

It was a warm summer evening the time, the only time, we were there. The windows were open, and we liked Raymonde's view of the Seine, and, just opposite, the towers of Notre Dame and the moon above them. Soon afterward, Raymonde died. We missed her terribly.

SIXTEEN

"*Notre Cher* Gide"

André Gide, as I have said, was one of my first subscribers, and remained a friend and supporter through the years. Adrienne and I saw a good deal of him one summer when we were down on the Mediterranean Coast at Hyères, where he joined us. Two days after our arrival at the little hotel on the beach, which I think Jules Romains, who lived in a tower up in the town, recommended to us, I looked up and saw Gide at a window. I said to Adrienne, "Gide is here," and she was much amused at the news.

Gide was fond of the sea and of swimming in it, and we now had our friend Gide splashing around with us in the warm blue water in front of the hotel. We appreciated his joining us. It was a real mark of his friendship. A great friend of his, Elizabeth Van Ruysselberghe, who had a place in the neighborhood, came often for a swim with us. She was the daughter of the Belgian painter Théo Van Ruysselberghe, an old friend of Gide's. She was a handsome, rather boyish girl, who, judging by her perfect English, must have been educated in England. Elizabeth became the mother of Gide's daughter Catherine; but that was later.

Elizabeth was an excellent swimmer. As for Gide and myself, it would have been hard to tell which was the worse.

Adrienne didn't swim at all. In a cork jacket and lifebelt, she simply floated upright close to the shore. Gide rowed me in a boat far out, where he wanted me to dive, though I had never tried diving and would have preferred not to begin in his presence. He watched me as I went off the end of the boat and flopped flat on the water; *"pas fameux!"* was his comment.

Sometimes Jules Romains came down from the town of Hyères, a mile above the beach, and had lunch with us. When it rained and we were shut indoors, Gide played Chopin for us on the hotel piano, an instrument that was somewhat affected by the sea air. He played with great feeling, but his playing was not as good as his writing.

After lunch on good days we all sat on the terrace in front of the hotel and drank our coffee and smoked. Gide was a great smoker. The little son of the hotelkeeper, a perfect pest, was always trying to climb up on Gide's knees, and Gide seemed to enjoy teasing him. Once when Gide went into the town, he brought back some chocolates that he knew were leftovers from the last winter season, and very moldy. He offered one to the little boy, who grabbed it, stuffed it into his mouth, and then, much to Gide's amusement, spit it out; the child kept on spitting and was quite vexed. Too bad, but the child was pestersome.

Actually, Gide was very kindhearted, and often young writers, stranded on his doorstep, were taken into his flat to share his meals. But any ties exasperated him and he shook them off rapidly. He would do anything for his friends, but not if they tried to pin him down. He could be cruel at times: for instance, so Larbaud told me, he never did turn up at the train he and Larbaud were to take to go to Italy one day. This was the sort of thing that hurt Larbaud very much.

Gide, as everyone knows, was quite interested in the movies for a time. He sold a lot of his books to finance a trip to the Congo with Marc Allégret to gather material for what was to be this now famous director's first picture. The film, with

Gide's scenario and Marc Allegret's photography, though it was rather amateurish and made in difficult circumstances, was admired by us all when it was shown at the Vieux Colombier theatre. The book Gide wrote about the Congo didn't exactly meet with the approval of officials. But Gide cared about neither official nor public opinion; he said what he pleased, whether in Russia or the colonies or at home.

Marc Allegret was a great friend of mine; he used to come often to the bookshop. Once he brought me a little turtle which he said was a present from Gide. Its name, it appeared, was Aglaé. I saw somewhere that Carl Van Vechten had a turtle named Aglaé; that must be the standard name for turtles.

Apropos of this gift of a turtle, I have a vague recollection of a story Gide told me about himself and one of his friends when they were schoolboys, and a trick they played on his concierge. He gave me leave to tell it in my memoirs.

It seems that his concierge had a medium-sized turtle in her loge. The boys got a larger one, and when the woman's back was turned removed her turtle and put the new one in its place. She didn't notice the difference. They went on getting larger and larger turtles. They heard the concierge exclaiming over the remarkable growth of her pet and wondering at the ways of turtles. The thing got enormous. It took up a great deal of room. Then it stopped growing, as the boys, though they searched all over Paris, couldn't find a larger one. Now they decided it was time for the turtle to shrink—which, to the poor concierge's dismay, it did, visibly. Finally, her turtle was a mere button.

The concierge disappeared shortly afterward, and upon their anxious inquiries, the boys were told that she had gone away for a rest.

My Friend Paul Valéry

I had the honor of knowing Paul Valéry, whom I also met at Adrienne Monnier's library, and often, after opening Shakespeare and Company, I had the joy of having him come in and sit down beside me to chat and to joke with me. Valéry was always joking.

As a young student under the spell of *La Jeune Parque*, I would never have believed that one day Valéry himself would be inscribing my copy, and that he himself would be coming to bring me each of his books as they appeared.

I loved Valéry, but then everybody who knew him loved him.

Valéry's visits to my bookshop were a great honor, but also great fun. In his very Valérian English, he teased me about my "patron." Once, seizing a volume of his works, he opened it at "The Phoenix and the Turtle," and asked, "Now, Sylvia, do you know what it's all about?" "No indeed." But it was nothing, he said, compared to Musset's lines which he had just been listening to at a poetry matinée at the Vieux Colombier. *"Les chants les plus beaux sont les chants de désespoir."* These lines, said Valéry, were, to him, completely obscure. "And they reproach me for my obscurity!"

Valéry told me something that had happened to him in London as a young man. It rained every day. He was alone and miserable in his dingy lodgings and, as he hinted, in very poor circumstances. One day he made up his mind he would commit suicide, but when he opened the cupboard to take out his revolver, he picked up a book that fell on the floor and sat down to read it. The author's name was Scholl; he was unable to recall the title. It was a humorous work; he read it through, and it amused him so much that when he had finished it he had lost all desire to commit suicide. How sad that Valéry couldn't remember the title! I could never even find the name Scholl in any catalogue.

Valéry's charm was unique, and so was his kindness. In spite of all the adulation and the "Cher Maître" that he exposed himself to in the upper circles he frequented, he was completely unaffected and treated everybody with the same bonhomie. He was always gay, even when he told you he had been so near to suicide.

A brilliant talker, he was a welcome figure in the *salons*, and quite frankly enjoyed them immensely. Yet Valéry was anything but a snob. When I teased him about it, he told me he found the tinkle of teacups and the chatter beneficial after his work. He rose every morning at six, made his own coffee, and began his work. He liked the early hour, when all was quiet in the house.

Once I said, teasing him, "You're all dressed up; you've been in a *salon*." Laughing, he put his finger through a big hole in the crown of his hat. He would mention some Princess. "You know her, Sylvia? . . . but she's an American!" I knew so few Princesses. "Now what would I do in a *salon?*" I would ask. And we both laughed a great deal over my funny ways.

In the middle twenties, our friend Valéry was elected to the Academy, the first among his friends to enter this institution. It was considered rather dusty at the time, and his colleagues disapproved, but each and every one of them entered the Academy as soon as their turns came.

Valéry attended the meetings at the Academy every Thursday—to get the hundred francs you were paid, he told me, jokingly, and also because it was only a short distance from the rue de l'Odéon. He always dropped in to see us on that day.

My sister Cyprian had the honor to be presented by Valéry with an original drawing by himself, but one, unfortunately, that she couldn't keep. Cyprian was in the bookshop one day when he dropped in. She was wearing a very short skirt and stockings that stopped at the knees. Valéry seized a pencil and drew a woman's head on one of her knees. He signed the work "P.V."

Bryher once asked Valéry to give her something for a special French number of her review, *Life and Letters Today*. Valéry asked me what I thought of giving her his essay "*Littérature.*" I thought it very appropriate; whereupon he made the frightening proposal that we translate his contribution together. A great honor, but one that I would have preferred to forgo in favor of a more competent translator.

Valéry, however, insisted on "our" doing it. If I got stuck, he said, all I had to do was to run over to the rue de Villejust (now rue Paul Valéry) for a consultation. Unfortunately, whenever I took his suggestion and ran over to the rue de Villejust to consult him, I found that I couldn't count on him as a collaborator. "Just what did you mean here?" I would ask. Pretending to look carefully at the passage, he would say, "What could I have meant to say?" or "I'm positive I never wrote that at all." Confronted with the text, he still denied any knowledge of it. Finally he would advise me simply to skip it. Now was that being a serious collaborator in "our" difficult task? At least I enjoyed these sessions with Valéry. The translation was to be signed by "Sylvia Beach and the Author," and he said "the Author" would take all the blame. I knew, and no getting out of it, that I was the murderer, a fellow murderer with "the Author," of one of Valéry's most fascinating works.

I was always very fond of Madame Valéry and also of her sister, the artist Paule Gobillard. They were the nieces of Berthe Morisot. They had sat to her for their portraits as children and young girls, and they grew up among the Impressionists. The walls of the apartment in the rue de Villejust were covered with the most precious Degas, Manets, Monets, Renoirs, and, of course, Berthe Morisots.

Valéry's younger son, François, was a great friend of mine. He was fair-haired, the only exception in a family of dark-haired people, though Valéry's daughter Agathe had beautiful blue'eyes, like his own. (Valéry's mother was Italian.) He seemed quite amused over the light coloring of his son François, and called him "this great Nordic brute."

The "Nordic brute" came often to my bookshop, to read the English poets and to tell me all the latest news in music. He studied composition at Nadia Boulanger's, almost lived at the place, from what he told me. All his pocket money was spent on concerts. The supply was limited, and once he supplemented it by selling one of his father's phonograph records. Valéry, incidentally, had quite a collection. Strange to say, he was a Wagnerian and, unlike Joyce, owned up to it.

I watched young François grow up. His English studies culminated in a thesis at the Sorbonne, and I was much interested to hear that the subject, *The Ring and the Book*, had been suggested by his father.

During the German Occupation, Valéry lectured on poetry at the Collège de France. The little lecture hall was crowded with Valérians. It wasn't always easy to follow him. His utterance was not very clear and now and again you lost the thread. Then I imagined, too, that he took a certain wicked pleasure in losing his hearers. These lectures were among the few things that counted during those days.

Madame Valéry invited me to lunch one day during the war. We had hardly sat down to table, with Francis Jourdain and Mademoiselle Paule Gobillard and François, when an air-raid alert was sounded. Valéry jumped up and rushed to the window and hung out to see the planes come over Paris, dropping bombs. The family seemed accustomed to this behavior. "Papa adores these raids," said François.

SEVENTEEN

Joyce's *Exiles*

Joyce's only dramatic work, at least the only one he claimed, was one of the first problems that he brought to me.

No sooner had he arrived in Paris than Lugné-Poe, one of the most esteemed theatrical managers in Paris, approached him with a contract in hand, authorizing the performance of *Exiles* at Le Théâtre de l'Oeuvre, of which Lugné-Poe was the director.

Joyce had no objection. On the contrary, he was delighted to have his play produced at the theatre that yearly put on a season of Ibsen, Joyce's god, as we know, at eighteen. He was looking forward to seeing Lugné-Poe's gifted wife, Susanne Depré, famous interpreter of Nora, in the role of Bertha.

The contract was signed. Time passed but nothing more was heard from Lugné-Poe, though he had seemed so eager to produce the play. Meanwhile, Joyce had word from a Monsieur Baernaert that he and a Madame Hélène Du Pasquier had finished a translation of *Exiles* which they hoped Hébertôt, director of the brilliant Théâtre des Champs Elysées would produce in those splendid surroundings. Hébertôt was disposed to accept *Exiles*, but he wanted first to be sure that the situation with Lugné-Poe was clear.

Joyce asked me to see Lugné-Poe and find out whether he

intended to do anything with *Exiles*. Lugné-Poe gave me an appointment at his theatre at eleven o'clock one morning. I spent some time chasing him around the wings and along drafty corridors before I finally caught up with him, and we sat down, panting, to talk about *Exiles*.

Lugné-Poe spoke very apologetically about his failure to produce Joyce's play. He had fully intended to put it on at Le Théâtre de l'Oeuvre, had even gone so far as to have it translated by his secretary, the playwright Natanson. He paused, and I waited. "You see," he said, "I have to earn my living. That's my problem. I must consider the demands of present-day theatregoers, and all they ask today is something that makes them laugh." I could see his point. Joyce's play was not at all funny, but neither, for that matter, was Ibsen. That's one thing about Bill Shakespeare, he let his clowns put a lot of gags in his plays.

Obviously, I couldn't urge Lugné-Poe to take the risk with *Exiles*. I had heard of his financial problems: they were probably even more acute by now. On the other hand, Joyce couldn't be expected to turn *Exiles* into a roaring comedy. When I reported the interview with Lugné-Poe to Joyce, his only comment was, "I should have made it funny. Richard should have had a peg leg!"

Instead of *Exiles*, Lugné-Poe produced a play by the Belgian playwright Fernand Crommelynck, *Le Cocu Magnifique* (*The Magnificent Cuckold*). The hero was a sort of very distant cousin, I thought, of Richard, but with the fun so piled on that the audiences at Le Théâtre de l'Oeuvre got all the laughs they wanted. *The Cuckold* ran for months.

Nothing now stood in the way of Hébertôt's plans for *Exiles*. The performances he put on at his theatre—music, ballet, and drama—were events nobody could afford to miss; or to attend, unless you were invited, as I was. In your seat you found Hébertôt's little bulletin announcing coming events: one of these, as I pointed out to the author, was *Exiles* by James Joyce. But for some reason Hébertôt never did put it on.

Louis Jouvet, who was running the little Comédie des Champs Elysées in a wing of the big theatre, became interested in Joyce's play, but since Joyce was not informed of it, Jouvet's failure to perform *Exiles* was a disappointment that was spared him. It was just as well Jouvet didn't attempt the part of Richard. His great roles—in *Knock* by Jules Romains, Molière's *Don Juan*, and *Le Tartuffe*—fitted him better.

Anyhow, Jouvet had the rights, and it was only years later, when they were planning to produce *Exiles* at the Comédie-Française, that he relinquished them, in Joyce's interest. That was the kind of man, a very good man, Jouvet was.

Joyce now showed me an enthusiastic letter from Copeau, director of the little Vieux Colombier theatre—"the Old Doves," as Gertrude Stein called it. Copeau seemed to be in such a hurry to perform the play that, at Joyce's request, I ran as fast I could to the Vieux Colombier, hoping to get there before the curtain went up on *Exiles*. Copeau was extremely cordial, expressing his great admiration for James Joyce and his play and assuring me that it would be the very next thing he produced; he saw himself already as Richard.

It really seemed reasonable to hope that Copeau would produce the play. Around him were grouped the best writers in France, and his audience was a highly perceptive one and inured to hardships. Copeau, I thought, should be able to get into Richard's skin and communicate the Joycean subtleties to his attentive listeners. Yes, I thought now we might hope.

Copeau's friends knew of his religious leanings, but I think some of them, especially those who had a play and were counting on him to produce it, were surprised to hear the news that Copeau had retired from the theatre to a life of contemplation in the country. This, so soon after my interview with him, when he had seemed so full of fervor for *Exiles*, did indeed astound me.

The next person calling for our play was a delightfully optimistic blonde woman. She arrived perspiring. When she got her breath, she told me that she had done a translation of James Joyce's *Exiles* without any difficulty, that she knew several theatres ready to put it right on, that she would keep me informed. Then off she ran.

This cheerful person was, so she told me, in aviation. Flying was her business; she occupied her spare time with the theatre. I enjoyed her "flying" visits, and her frequent letters, in a tall handwriting. She blew from airfield to bookshop and around theatres, and the news was always good. But neither Joyce nor I was much surprised when the whirring died away and the visits of our flying friend ceased.

Just before World War II began, an attractive young woman, a compatriot of Joyce's and the wife of an actor-member—"*Sociétaire*," they call it—at the Comédie-Française, began to frequent my bookshop. Joyce's works interested her particularly, and she told me one day of her great desire to have *Exiles* performed at the Comédie-Française. She herself had translated it (one more translation!). A friend of hers had helped her to adapt it for the French stage. She felt sure that it would be accepted, and her husband, Marcel Dessonnes, was already studying the part of Richard.

This seemed promising. The enthusiastic Madame Dessonnes hurried back and forth. She brought her husband to tell me how much he admired *Exiles* and was looking forward to playing Richard himself. I was invited to see him in various roles, and he was an admirable artist.

Finally, because there were certain problems that I thought they should take up with the author, I arranged a meeting with Joyce at the bookshop.

The problems were easily settled. One of them was whether Joyce would object to the necessary adaptations for the French stage. He assured Madame Dessonnes that he wouldn't interfere with the performance of his play—that was not his business. The kiss was brought up. She asked him if he would be willing to let her modify it for the Comédie-Française. There were many *jeunes filles* in the audience. The kiss would never do; in fact, she had been told that not an audience in Paris would stand for it.

Joyce, much amused at these French reactions to his kiss, said she had carte blanche for that and anything else in his play.

I was happy to think that we were to see *Exiles* in the Number One theatre in Paris, and quite hopeful. Joyce was pleased, but he was not as hopeful as I was. He predicted that something would happen to prevent the performance of his play.

The "something" that Joyce predicted was the war. As it turned out, *Exiles* was not performed in Paris till fifteen years later, in 1954. This time it was Mrs. Jenny Bradley's excellent translation, actually the first to be made, she told me. It was performed at the Théâtre Gramont, and was so well done that I regretted that Joyce was no longer there to see it.

Ben W. Huebsch, American publisher of *Exiles*, attended its first performance, at the Neighborhood Playhouse, in New York in 1925. He sent me a copy of his letter to Helen Arthur, who produced the play. I think Mr. Huebsch has summed up once and for all the difficulties of bringing *Exiles* and an audience together. He has very kindly permitted me to quote from his letter. After praising the production and the actors at the Neighborhood Playhouse, he said:

As I see it, the great difficulty of putting on a play of that kind lies in conveying to an audience the unspoken thoughts and emotions of the characters and in making the actual speeches an index of such hidden thoughts without dulling the subtlety of the words. The difficulty becomes complex in that each character must be realized from the point of view of what he permits the audience to hear and from what he permits the audience to infer, and more complex in that the audience must get a notion of what the characters think of each other without depending entirely upon what they say to each other.

To present a crisis in the conflict of souls for an evening's entertainment (that sounds raw, but most people do go to the theater for entertainment) is a very hard task and particularly so in such a play as *Exiles* which does not act itself but requires actors. I should think that the real actor would love Joyce's parts just because they are so severe a test. You cannot walk through those parts—you have to act or fail.

In 1955, I heard *Exiles* over the Paris Radio, in French. It was extremely well done. René Lalou introduced it to the listeners; the part of Richard was taken admirably by Pierre Blanchard.

"A.L.P."

Anna Livia Plurabelle, or "A.L.P.," as we called her for short, the heroine of *Finnegans Wake*, Joyce's "Work in Progress," gave me some trouble.

Wyndham Lewis, on one of his visits to Paris, mentioned to Joyce that he expected to bring out a new review shortly, which was to be the successor to *Tyro*. Would Joyce give him, as soon as possible, a piece of his new work? Joyce promised to do so. He thought this a good time, and Lewis's magazine a good place, for his heroine to make her debut. She was now ready to leave the workshop. Her creator picked her up and brushed the shavings off her skirts; and I packed her off to Wyndham Lewis. Joyce, meanwhile, went off to Belgium.

We received no acknowledgment of the receipt of the text and no news at all from Lewis. Joyce, in Brussels, waiting impatiently and bothered by his eyes, could bear the suspense no longer and wrote a letter to Lewis with his biggest blackest pencil. He sent it to me, asking me to copy it and send it to Lewis as a letter from me. I did so.

I had no reply to "my" letter. But in time I received No. 1 of a new review edited by Wyndham Lewis called *The Enemy*. Joyce's text was not in it. All the space was taken

up by a violent attack on Joyce's new work by Wyndham
Lewis.

Joyce was really hurt by this attack. He was disappointed,
too, over the lost opportunity to introduce a member of the
Earwicker family to London readers.

The next editor who asked for "A.L.P." was a young Englishman named Edgell Rickward. He was preparing the first
number of *his* new review, *The Calendar*. He wrote offering
"the hospitality of our pages to Joyce, the greatest power of
the present generation."

I promised him "A.L.P." but warned him that he would
have to wait for it until after Mr. Eliot had published in the
Criterion a piece that came earlier in the work. He said he
would tell the subscribers, who had come in flocks on hearing
that the *Calendar* was bringing out in its first number an extract from Joyce's new book, to hold on.

The *Criterion* appeared, and I packed off "A.L.P." immediately to the *Calendar*. I got a delighted letter of acknowledgment from the editor; then a mortified, crestfallen one.
The printers had refused to set up the passage beginning "two
boys in their breeches" and ending with "blushing and looking askance at her." Very respectfully, the *Calendar*'s editor
asked Mr. Joyce's permission to delete this passage from his
text.

Very reluctantly, I replied that Mr. Joyce regretted the
inconvenience over his contribution but could not discuss any
alteration of his text—and would Mr. Rickward please return it.

Till now, Adrienne Monnier had published only French
texts in *Le Navire d'Argent*, but she immediately invited
"A.L.P." to come, just as she was, in English, aboard the
Silver Ship. That is how this piece of Joyce's new work first
appeared in a French review.

Adrienne found "A.L.P." very amusing and helped to translate it into French when it was published in the *Nouvelle
Revue Française*. Everybody turned to and helped, including

Joyce himself, and the translation was recited by Adrienne in a reading at her library—her second Joyce reading.

Joyce was extremely anxious to introduce his heroine to readers in the United States. Aiming high, I sent her off to the *Dial*, hoping its editor, Marianne Moore, would find her attractive.

I was glad to get word that the *Dial* had accepted the work, but it turned out that this was a mistake. It had come in when Miss Moore was away, and she was reluctant to publish it. The *Dial* didn't back out altogether. I was told, however, that the text would have to be considerably cut down to meet the requirements of the magazine. Now Joyce might have considered the possibility of expanding a work of his, but never, of course, of whittling it down. On the other hand, I couldn't blame the *Dial* for its prudence in dealing with a piece so full of rivers that they might have been overflooded at 152 West Thirteenth Street.

I was sorry about "A.L.P.'s" failure to make the *Dial*. Joyce, who was still in Belgium, was not surprised. "Why did you not bet with me?" he wrote. "I should have won something." He added that he regretted the loss of a "strategical position." Joyce always looked upon his *Finnegans Wake* as a kind of battle.

Two Records

In 1924, I went to the office of His Master's Voice in Paris to ask them if they would record a reading by James Joyce from *Ulysses*. I was sent to Piero Coppola, who was in charge of musical records, but His Master's Voice would agree to record the Joyce reading only if it were done at my expense. The record would not have their label on it, nor would it be listed in their catalogue.

Some recording of writers had been done in England and in

France as far back as 1913. Guillaume Apollinaire had made some recordings which are preserved in the archives of the Musée de la Parole. But in 1924, as Coppola said, there was no demand for anything but music. I accepted the terms of His Master's Voice: thirty copies of the recording to be paid for on delivery. And that was the long and the short of it.

Joyce himself was anxious to have this record made, but the day I took him in a taxi to the factory in Billancourt, quite a distance from town, he was suffering with his eyes and very nervous. Luckily, he and Coppola were soon quite at home with each other, bursting into Italian to discuss music. But the recording was an ordeal for Joyce, and the first attempt was a failure. We went back and began again, and I think the *Ulysses* record is a wonderful performance. I never hear it without being deeply moved.

Joyce had chosen the speech in the Aeolus episode, the only passage that could be lifted out of *Ulysses*, he said, and the only one that was "declamatory" and therefore suitable for recital. He had made up his mind, he told me, that this would be his only reading from *Ulysses*.

I have an idea that it was not for declamatory reasons alone that he chose this passage from Aeolus. I believe that it expressed something he wanted said and preserved in his own voice. As it rings out—"he lifted his voice above it boldly"—it is more, one feels, than mere oratory.

The *Ulysses* recording was "very bad," according to my friend C. K. Ogden. *The Meaning of Meaning* by Mr. Ogden and I. A. Richards was much in demand at my bookshop. I had Mr. Ogden's little Basic English books, too, and sometimes saw the inventor of this strait jacket for the English language. He was doing some recording of Bernard Shaw and others at the studio of the Orthological Society in Cambridge and was interested in experimenting with writers, mainly, I suspect, for language reasons. (Shaw was on Ogden's side, couldn't see what Joyce was after when there were already more words in the English language than one knew what to do with.) Mr. Ogden boasted that he had the two biggest recording machines in the world at his Cambridge studio and told me to send Joyce over to him for a real recording. And Joyce went over to Cambridge for the recording of "Anna Livia Plurabelle."

So I brought these two together, the man who was liberating and expanding the English language and the one who was condensing it to a vocabulary of five hundred words. Their experiments went in opposite directions, but that didn't prevent them from finding each other's ideas interesting. Joyce would have starved on five or six hundred words, but he was quite amused by the Basic English version of "Anna Livia Plurabelle" that Ogden published in the review *Psyche*. I thought Ogden's "translation" deprived the work of all its beauty, but Mr. Ogden and Mr. Richards were the only persons I knew about whose interest in the English language equaled that of Joyce, and when the Black Sun Press published the little volume *Tales Told of Shem and Shaun*, I suggested that C. K. Ogden be asked to do the preface.

How beautiful the "Anna Livia" recording is, and how amusing Joyce's rendering of an Irish washerwoman's brogue! This is a treasure we owe to C. K. Ogden and Basic English. Joyce, with his famous memory, must have known Anna Livia by heart. Nevertheless, he faltered at one place and, as in the *Ulysses* recording, they had to begin again.

Ogden gave me both the first and second versions. Joyce gave me the immense sheets on which Ogden had had "Anna Livia" printed in huge type so that the author—his sight was growing dimmer—could read it without effort. I wondered where Mr. Ogden had got hold of such big type, until my friend Maurice Saillet, examining it, told me that the corresponding pages in the book had been photographed and much enlarged. The "Anna Livia" recording was on both sides of the disc; the passage from *Ulysses* was contained on one. And it was the only recording from *Ulysses* that Joyce would consent to.

How I regret that, owing to my ignorance of everything pertaining to recording, I didn't do something about preserving the "master." This was the rule with such records, I was told, but for some reason the precious "master" of the recording from *Ulysses* was destroyed. Recording was done in a rather primitive manner in those days, at least at the Paris branch of His Master's Voice, and Ogden was right, the *Ulysses* record was not a success technically. All the same, it is the only recording of Joyce himself reading from *Ulysses*, and it is my favorite of the two.

The *Ulysses* record was not at all a commercial venture. I handed over most of the thirty copies to Joyce for distribution among his family and friends, and sold none until, years later, when I was hard up, I did set and get a stiff price for one or two I had left.

Discouraged by the experts at the office of the successors to His Master's Voice in Paris, and those of the B.B.C. in London, I gave up the attempt to have the record "re-pressed"—which I believe is the term. I gave my permission to the B.B.C. to make a recording of my record, the last I possessed, for the purpose of broadcasting it on W. R. Rodgers' Joyce program, in which Adrienne Monnier and I took part.

Anyone who wishes to hear the *Ulysses* record can do so at the Musée de la Parole in Paris, where, thanks to the suggestion of my California friend Philias Lalanne, Joyce's reading is preserved among those of some of the great French writers.

EIGHTEEN

Pomes Penyeach

In 1927 I published *Pomes Penyeach.*

Every once in a while, Joyce wrote a poem, and usually, I believe, "threw it out." Some he put aside, and in 1927 he brought me thirteen of these and asked me if I would care to print them: a baker's dozen to be sold for one shilling, like the wares of the old apple woman on the bridge over the Liffey. He called them *Pomes Penyeach.* That's all they were worth, in his opinion; and, of course, "Pomes" was a play on the French *Pommes.* He wanted the cover to be exactly the green of the Calville apple, a peculiarly delicate, greenish shade— which proves that Joyce could distinguish shades of color in spite of his diminished sight.

I went to the English printer in Paris, Herbert Clarke, who had some pretty type. I explained to him that the author wanted a cheap-looking little booklet to be sold for one bob. He turned out, reluctantly, a miserable little green pamphlet. He thought it looked "pharmaceutical." I saw that Joyce himself was regretful, though he would have stuck to his guns. It was I who couldn't bear to be the publisher of such a little monster. I liked the *Pomes*, too, and wanted them nicely turned out.

Clarke said he could do a better job with boards than with

paper covers, but then it would cost me more and I couldn't sell it for a shilling—six francs fifty at the rate of exchange in 1927. I ordered the boards, and sold it for a shilling to conform with the title. It was a pretty little book. Thirteen large paper copies were printed for Joyce and his friends, and they were signed, not with his full name, but only his initials.

Joyce wanted not only his poems, but his other works, too, sold at low prices that those he considered his real readers could pay. But they were often published in a particular manner and regardless of expense to his publishers. If he had paid more attention to our problems, it would have made it easier for us. But this was a matter to which he was completely indifferent. So, either you run your publishing business far away, where your writer can't get at it, or you publish right alongside of him—and have much more fun—and much more expense.

The people to whom Joyce gave the thirteen large paper copies were: No. 1, S. B.; No. 2, Harriet Weaver; No. 3, Arthur Symons; No. 4, Larbaud; No. 5, Georgio; No. 6, Lucia; No. 7, Adrienne Monnier; No. 8, Claude Sykes; No. 9, A. Mac-Leish; No. 10, Eugene Jolas; No. 11, Elliot Paul; No. 12, Mrs. Myron Nutting; and No. 13, J. J. himself.

"*P. P.*" as Joyce called it, was a pleasant volume to handle in contrast to *Ulysses*. It was "handled" in London by the Poetry Bookshop, where it had a warm welcome. But I think, on the whole, the appearance of such an unassuming thing from Joyce's pen rather disconcerted his readers. It wasn't "great poetry"—but who said it was? Joyce knew his limitations as a poet. He asked me if I didn't think he expressed himself better as a prose writer. To him, great poetry was that of Yeats, which he was always reciting to me and to which he was always trying to convert me—a waste of time, for I was much more interested in Valéry, Perse, and Michaux, and, of course, in Marianne Moore and T. S. Eliot.

What attracted me in Joyce's little verses was a certain mystery present in all his work, the strange presence of Joyce himself. And these "Pomes," particularly "On the Beach at Fontana" and "A Prayer," affected me deeply.

It was an immense joy for him when thirteen composers set *Pomes Penyeach* to music and the Oxford University Press brought them out as a tribute to James Joyce. This production, with a portrait by Augustus John, Editor's Note by Herbert Hughes, Prologue by James Stephens, and Epilogue by Arthur Symons, appeared on "St. Patrick's Eve," 1932; and, a funny coincidence, it was printed by the Sylvan Press. I have seldom seen anything that pleased Joyce as much as this "Joyce book." I suppose Joyce was not the only writer who liked an occasional tribute, but he was perhaps the only one who got a musical tribute. Like his fellow writers, he resented criticism. In fact, it was "like a penknife in my heart," as the nursery rhyme says. Joyce was seriously wounded by Ezra's contemptuous remark on receiving the little volume of *Pomes Penyeach* that it was "the sort of poetry to be kept in the family Bible."

Soon after *Pomes Penyeach* was published, Arthur Symons dropped in. I called up Joyce, and as soon as he heard that Symons was in the bookshop, he said he would come immediately. Joyce always remembered Symons' article praising *Chamber Music* when it first appeared.

Arthur Symons was taking a holiday on the Continent after a breakdown, and was accompanied by a benevolent-looking bearded man, who was no other than Dr. Havelock Ellis. They were a strangely assorted pair of traveling companions: Symons, a pale fragile sort of poet, with a complexion that looked made up, and Havelock Ellis, with his Apostle's head, out of which had come all those volumes on sex to enlighten a whole generation puzzled over their problems. My friendship with Ellis was on a business basis; I was the Paris agent for *The Psychology of Sex*.

Dr. Ellis and Arthur Symons came one day to take me out to lunch at a restaurant. Sitting at table between these two winged creatures was an experience as curious as it could be. Their menus were characteristic. Symons, an epicure, conferred with the waiter and the sommelier and won the respect of both by his choice of *"cuisinés"* dishes and the right wines. Dr. Ellis said he would like vegetables, and no wine, thank you, just water. The waiter was a long time procuring these articles. My own menu was something between the two extremes.

The conversation was supplied by Symons. Neither Dr. Ellis nor I could get in a word, nor cared to. I never was able to give my attention to a meal and a conversation at the same time. If the food is nice, no other thoughts should intrude; if there is a conversation, whether on business or on art, one listens attentively, and how can one do that and at the same time enjoy nice food? I always noticed that the French at table wouldn't discuss anything, except perhaps the food, till after the second helping, when one could begin to think of something else.

The subject that interested Symons—after Joyce, who interested him very much—was the two pairs of shoes he had lost on his trip. They had fallen out of the back of the car he was traveling in down in the South of France, he told me.

Besides Joyce, we had Blake in common, with the difference that Symons was a great authority on Blake whereas I was only a Blake lover. At the bookshop he examined my two drawings that I had purchased from Elkin Mathews. He pronounced them authentic, and thought they might be studies for Blair's *Grave*. They were good examples, he said, and he congratulated me on my luck in acquiring them. Another connoisseur of Blake, Darrell Figgis, the Irish writer whose life ended so tragically, also looked at these drawings and said there was no doubt of their authenticity.

Our Exag

My third and last Joyce publication was in 1929. It was the volume with the long, long title, *Our Exagmination Round his*

Factification for Incamination of Work in Progress, a title that got clipped down in subsequent editions of this work.

The title, of course, was Joyce's; perhaps, too, the "Litter" at the end. The book was composed of twelve studies of Joyce's new "Work in Progress" by twelve writers: Samuel Beckett, Marcel Brion, Frank Budgen, Stuart Gilbert, Eugene Jolas, Victor Llona, Robert McAlmon, Thomas McGreevy, Elliot Paul, John Rodker, Robert Sage, and William Carlos Williams. These were writers who had been watching "Work in Progress" from the beginning, each seeing it from his own angle, but interested in Joyce's experiment, and friendly toward it.

Joyce thought an unfavorable article should be included in the volume. This wasn't easy to find in the immediate neighborhood, where everybody I knew was strongly pro "Work in Progress." However, I had heard one of my customers, a journalist, express herself strongly against the new Joycean technique, and I asked her if she would be willing to contribute an article to the publication, saying, rather rashly, she could go as far as she liked. This lady wrote the article entitled "Writes a Common Reader," and she came down so hard on Joyce that I was quite displeased with "G. V. L. Slingsby," as she signed herself, a name taken from Lear's "The Jumblies." It was not even very good as criticism, I must say.

About this time, the postman brought me a huge funny-looking envelope with the name of the sender, "Vladimir Dixon," and the address, "c/o Brentano's," on the back of it. It contained a rather clever take-off of the Joycean manner, and it so amused Joyce that he thought I should certainly ask the fellow to let me include it in the volume of *Our Exag.* That is how his "Litter" appeared as the fourteenth appreciation in our book.

I never, as far as I know, had the pleasure of meeting Mr. Dixon, but I suspected him of being no other than "The Germ's Choice" himself. It seemed to me that the handwriting of Dixon had one or two little Joycean characteristics. I may have been mistaken.

Joyce always had a strong desire to share, to a certain extent, his ideas with others; the teacher's instinct was also strong in him. *Our Exagmination* was an indirect outlet for this. He loved to guide and even mislead his tourists.

My contribution to *Our Exag* was the design on the cover: a circle formed by the names of the contributors turning the subject "round his factification." I got it from the paper enclosed in a publication called *Astronomy-1928,* probably an annual, that was sent to me by a certain W. L. Bass of Branchville, New Jersey. It had a kind of clockface on it with, instead of my twelve authors, the twelve hours.

When Mr. Eliot suggested that Messrs. Faber and Faber take over *Our Exagmination,* I thought indeed the best thing that could happen to it would be to follow in *Finnegans Wake.*

In the early stages of "Work in Progress," Joyce had asked me to be the eventual publisher of the book. I was beginning to feel rather exhausted by my Joycean-Shakespeare and Company labors, and less and less able to keep up with Joyce's financial requirements. It was a great relief to think that Miss Weaver and Mr. Eliot were going to take care of *Finnegans Wake.*

Pirates

I wouldn't be surprised to hear that the pirating of Joyce's work began with the theft of his pamphlet on Parnell, which he wrote at the age of nine. The first I heard of pirates boarding Joyce's craft was when an unauthorized edition of *Chamber Music* was brought out in Boston in 1918. Much more serious was the rape of *Ulysses* in 1926. It took years, and publication by Random House, to restore the book to its author.

Ulysses was not protected by copyright in the United States. To secure the copyright, a book had to be set up and printed in our country, an impossibility for a banned work. Of course, no reputable American publisher dreamed of taking advantage of the situation of Joyce and of innumerable other European writers. But footpads were lurking.

In 1926, full-page advertisements appeared in English and American weeklies announcing the publication of *Ulysses* in a magazine called *Two Worlds* and of a "new un-named work by James Joyce" in a magazine called *Two Worlds Quarterly*, both under the editorship of Samuel Roth. Still another publication of his, *Beau*, was to publish works by T. S. Eliot. Contributors to these periodicals included, according to the announcement, practically all the best writers of the period. Just help yourself.

There was a great deal of indignation among the involuntary contributors to Samuel Roth's publications. Eliot, like Joyce, was a pet victim—the first number of *Beau* was entirely devoted to his work. He wrote to me immediately to say that he would join us in protesting against Roth's activities, and letters from him and from myself were printed in many papers and magazines. And now someone was printing *Ulysses* in book form. The spurious edition, though it bore the imprint of Shakespeare and Company and the printer's name, was easily recognizable if you were familiar with the authentic one—the text was altered, the paper and type were not the same. Thus, for the next few years, some pirate succeeded in putting into his pocket the earnings of a writer who had not only spent a long time on his work and was losing his eyesight, but whose financial problems were becoming more and more serious.

A visitor from the Middle West, a fellow bookseller, told me how "bookleggers" supplied shops with their wares. A truck stopped at the door. The driver, always a different one, asked how many copies of *Ulysses*—or *Lady Chatterley's Lover*—were wanted. The bookseller could have ten or more at $5—to be sold for $10. The driver dumped his books and was gone.

Joyce thought I should go to the United States and do

something about the pirating. But I couldn't abandon Shakespeare and Company, and, anyway, only publication in the United States could put an end to the pirating. I did think that every effort should be made to call attention to what was going on. We had a consultation with our friends in Paris, and it was decided that a protest should be drawn up, bearing the signatures of as many writers as we could get in touch with, and given to the press all over the world.

The protest was written by Ludwig Lewissohn, and revised by Archibald MacLeish to insure its legality. I had copies printed, and everyone we knew signed it and helped me to get signatures. Besides the writers in Paris at the time, I thought we should ask authors all over Europe to sign—English, German, Austrian, Italian, Spanish, Scandinavian. Joyce was particularly anxious to get the signatures of the Scandinavians, and seemed to think that the whole thing would go to pieces if I didn't track down Olaf Bull, the Norwegian poet. (With the help of Joyce's Danish teacher, I succeeded in doing so.) Joyce and everyone else gave me suggestions, but I must say that most of the names, including the French Academicians, were my own idea. I put in a good many hours searching out addresses, and, to almost every writer, I sent a personal letter. I received many interesting replies. Many of the signers were fellow victims of piracy and felt strongly about it. I have carefully preserved these letters, and the signatures make a sort of roll call of the writers of our time. As the replies poured in, Joyce peered at them over my shoulder, and the "banned writer" showed a touching appreciation of the cordiality of his fellow authors.

The protest was printed in newspapers everywhere and in many reviews and magazines. The *Humanist* devoted a page to it and reproduced some of the signatures. At the request of the editor, I had the ones he chose reproduced by my printer in Paris, and I still have a box full of the little plates. Incidentally, the designation *"de l'Académie Française,"* which was supposed to appear below the signature of one of the

French Academicians—several of them signed the protest—somehow got attached to the name of Ernest Hemingway. But nobody protested.

Roth was very wroth over the protest and accused "that vicious virago, Joyce's secretary Sylvia Beach" of including some dead writers among the signers. This was something he might have done himself, I suppose, but I was not guilty of it. The letters in my dossier are sufficient proof of their authenticity. I must say, however, that one or two of my signers who were aged and ailing did die shortly afterward. The only writer who refused to sign the protest was Ezra Pound. That was just like Ezra.

In spite of all my efforts, the exploitation of *Ulysses* went on.

Once, on Staten Island, I noticed a big sign guaranteeing to rid you of "The Pest of the Month." Joyce and I should have subscribed to the service. Someone was always grabbing something. Joyce was continually the prey of pirates. Invariably, they declared themselves to be "great admirers"; and proved it by their acts. He had his "admirers" as far away as Japan; I was sent four fat volumes of the Tokyo *Ulysses* with greetings from the publishers! And when I protested against these thefts, I was usually accused of being grasping.

Pomes Penyeach was picked like a daisy by a young publisher in the Middle West, who seemed to be in such haste to bring it out that he couldn't wait until he had the author's permission, or mine. I had just published it when I got the disquieting news from an admirer of these poems in Cleveland that an edition was about to appear. I asked my father to have the necessary number of copies printed at the Princeton University Press to secure the copyright in Washington. But the unauthorized edition—private and of course and as usual "not for sale"—probably got there first; and the author never got his twelve pennies per copy. *Pomes Penylesseach*.

NINETEEN

Successor to *Ulysses*

I don't know when Joyce first began to think of *Finnegans Wake*, but, since creation with him never ceased, Mr. Earwicker must have taken over from Mr. Bloom the very next day after *Ulysses* was finished. As soon as *Ulysses* was off his hands, he lost interest in it as a book if not as an investment, and said he wished people wouldn't talk to him on the subject. He talked willingly about his new work, and I followed it with him step by step, as much interested in the H.C.E. family as I had been in the Ulyssean characters. He explained everything in signs and drawings and alphabets as we went along, and I found all of his ideas so interesting, amusing, and convincing that by the time the whole book appeared I was at home in it and inured to his way of writing, which he called "working in layers," instead of the flat method adopted by others. He thought that the way a man was usually described left everything out. About language, he didn't agree with Shaw that the English vocabulary was large enough without inventing any more words. Joyce was for having all the fun you wanted with the word game, and didn't see why there was a need to set any limits; "*mesure*" as the French understand it was not consistent with the character of the creator of *Ulysses* and, particularly, of *Finnegans Wake*. But he said maybe he was wrong, and that maybe the other way was best. <u>Only he felt others didn't have half as good a time with words as they might.</u>

The tendency in England at the time Joyce was beginning his new work was to keep the language within bounds. English books told you what you could say and what you couldn't, what strangers could be introduced into the language on a strict quota, what was American and what was slang, and so on. Mr. C. K. Ogden's Basic English, which gave you five or six hundred words to live on, was amusing in contrast to the overflowing Joycean vocabulary.

Joyce related to me the story of how he happened to choose the giant theme in his new work. He had asked Miss Harriet Weaver to suggest a subject, and she had told him about a certain "Giant's Grave" in Cornwall. Thereupon he rushed right over to Cornwall to have a look. Eugene Jolas heard the same story from Joyce's own lips some time later. As early as 1922, I think, Joyce seemed to be interested in giants; he said to me that what particularly struck him in Frank Harris's *Oscar Wilde* was the preface by Bernard Shaw in which he speaks of the gigantism of Wilde.

I have a photograph of Joyce wearing his cross-Channel cap on his way to Bognor in 1923 to interview the "Giant."

In 1924 he was looking over the menhirs at Carnac with Auguste Morel, the translator of *Ulysses*. On a postcard from them both he speaks of "Cyclops."

Then it was rivers. During the summer of 1925 he was plunging into rivers. I got a postcard from Bordeaux: "Garonne, Garonne!" But heaven knows how many rivers Joyce was acquainted with personally. He was in love with the Seine, his "Anna Sequana," I know. I remember that Adrienne and I took him in our Citroën to a spot he wanted to visit up the Seine, where some waterworks was situated that he wanted "to have a look at." He sat on the bank, once he had inspected the waterworks, and gazed intently at the river and all the different objects floating in it.

For someone whose sight was failing, Joyce could see a surprising number of things. But I think that as his sight diminished, his hearing developed so that he lived more and more in a world of sounds, so, *Finnegans Wake*, to be comprehensible, must be heard by the reader. Even in his earliest work, Joyce was always harping on sound. His sight as a child, as one remembers, was weak.

The very mention of war made Joyce tremble, and he disliked even any quarreling around him, saying, "I'm a peaceful person." Yet, toward 1926 he was taking up battles. I got for him Edward S. Creasy's *Fifteen Decisive Battles of the World: 12 Plans*. He had a look at them, then off he and his family went to have a look at Waterloo with its "museyroom: tip." The Joycean jumble of battlefields, the "Lipoleums," on their "white arses," with their boots and cocked hats, is one of the most amusing passages in his work. He wrote again from Belgium the following year; in a letter dated "Waterloo Day," he tells of the waiter at his hotel recommending some wine that was "*oen bloem*" ("ane bloom"). Joyce conducted the battle of the books like a veritable campaign. I think he was sometimes discouraged by a certain lack of interest, if not downright hostility, to his second great work. What, I wonder, were his musings in the "museyroom" at Waterloo?

I think Joyce sometimes enjoyed misleading his readers. He said to me that history was like that parlor game where someone whispers something to the person next to him, who repeats it not very distinctly to the next person, and so on until, by the time the last person hears it, it comes out completely transformed. Of course, as he explained to me, the meaning in *Finnegans Wake* is obscure because it is a "nightpiece." I think, too, that, like the author's sight, the work is often blurred.

When Joyce was engaged on his new work, he came in for some criticism, quite to his surprise, I think, on the part of those who had been in sympathy with his efforts in the *Ulysses* period. I remember Harold Monro saying to me in

1919 that he thought Joyce should have stopped after *A Portrait of the Artist;* perhaps some of the *Ulysses* admirers thought he should have stopped after that.

Joyce could always count on Mr. T. S. Eliot's friendly encouragement and always came back from his visits to him considerably cheered, but it was not so with some of his fellow penmen.

James and Two Johns

Two singers, both of them compatriots of Joyce's, contributed to the making of Shem and Shaun in *Finnegans Wake.*

Early in the "progress" of this "work," the author fell under the spell of John MacCormack. As young men in Dublin, they had appeared on the same program at a concert, and James ever since had been fascinated by John. He had followed the career of John MacCormack step by step. Joyce never quite lost the illusion that he might have been a singer himself. He read all the newspaper accounts of MacCormack's doings, his love affairs, his tennis playing, his way of dressing and his curly hairdo. Little did MacCormack know that he was sitting for his portrait to James Joyce.

Joyce talked so much about John MacCormack that finally I got all his records. I liked *"Una Furtiva Lagrima."* Adrienne doted on "Dear Old Pal of Mine." It was "Molly Brannigan," of course, that interested Joyce. He asked me if I hadn't noticed a striking resemblance between his own voice and MacCormack's. It may have been due to a certain Irish timbre, but there was indeed a resemblance between the two voices.

Molly Bloom Brannigan, however, had now been replaced by Anna Livia Plurabelle, and it was this lady's son Shaun who was emerging in "Work in Progress." Of course many people contributed odds and ends to Joyce's characters, but these were only the accessories. One figure dominated. When I attended a recital of John MacCormack's with the Joyces, I felt I had already met him as "Shaun the Post."

MacCormack's lovely tenor voice and his great art were irresistible, and I applauded him almost as enthusiastically as did Joyce. He asked me if I had noticed MacCormack's pigeon-toed way of walking on and off the platform, and if I didn't think him charming with his chubbiness, his curls, and his manner of bowing. Indeed I did. But what I found amazing, and touching, was Joyce's infatuation, the extraordinary emotions he displayed as he listened to him.

Joyce was interested in singing, but MacCormack didn't seem to take much interest in writing. He accepted Joyce's admiration along with that of his other fans, and I thought he was not particularly concerned with anybody but himself. And Joyce, too, now that he had finished "Shaun the Post" could do without MacCormack. So I heard no more about him.

Another singer, also a fellow Irishman and he, too, named John, was far more perceptive, and Joyce's interest in him far exceeded any he had displayed in MacCormack. An account of this episode in Joyce's life, by Ellsworth Mason and Richard Ellmann, has been published in the Northwestern University review, *The Analyst*.

Those of us who knew James Joyce and observed his fascination with the opera and operatic stars might compare *Finnegans Wake* to a vast opera, with its Tristans and Isoldes, its William Tells—a sort of Joycean Ring away up there in his particular "Veiled Horror." Of course this is only one aspect of a book with everybody and everything in it, but one that seems to me very Joycean.

I followed closely, with Eugene and Maria Jolas and Mr. and Mrs. Stuart Gilbert, the Joyce-Sullivan affair, one of the most extraordinary in the Joyce history.

The Joyces were great operagoers. They had gone a great deal to the opera in Trieste and, like the Italians, they were exacting with singers, kept a close watch on every note and were relentless toward anyone guilty of shirking the high C. Joyce told me that the last Italian tenor able to cope with William Tell had died a hundred years ago, and, until he could be replaced, *William Tell* would not be performed in Italy. The Italians were still waiting for a Tell, and so was Joyce.

Now Joyce needed the help of Tell with *Finnegans Wake* and would have liked to listen to him every night. Unfortunately, the tenor at the Paris Opera House, the Guillaume Tell whose mellow tones and charming art the French audiences admired, was disapproved of by Joyce; he fell short of the high C, and Joyce was so annoyed with him that he told me he had to give up attending performances of *Guillaume Tell*.

Then one day, as he scrutinized the bills posted up at the Opera, he saw a new name in the place of the usual Tell, an Irish Tell, John Sullivan. Greatly excited, he ran up the steps to the box office and booked four seats for the performance that night. The members of the Joyce family—"there they were the four of them" in the front row—listened for the first time to the grand voice of John Sullivan, with the score, like the text of *Ulysses*, "complete as written." Joyce was carried away by Sullivan's voice. He said to me that it was cleansing and reminded him of the men that came for the garbage in the early morning. He attended every performance of *Guillaume Tell*, applauded Sullivan exuberantly from his seat in the front row, and got up to call him back many times. The little old lady ushers with their back lace caps joined in the applause, Joyce having tipped them so generously that they would have applauded anybody, and Joyce's friends all over the house formed a "claque." We all attended performances of *Guillaume Tell*. We all admired John Sullivan; Joyce filled the theater with Sullivan's admirers, and, of course, with his own admirers. I happened to like *William Tell*. Others, non-opera-goers as a rule, "attended there as they were bid" but reluctantly.

John Sullivan, a fine big handsome man, looked like a god and had a voice of enormous range, one to ring out from Tell's native mountaintops. He was an indifferent actor, though, and didn't seem much interested in the character he represented. He had a businesslike air, never played to the gallery. On stage, Sullivan lacked warmth and MacCormack's charm, and he had nothing of the theatrical about him.

James Joyce and John Sullivan both suffered from what they fancied was persecution. See Joyce's "From a Banned Writer to a Banned Singer." (Actually, I think the banning of *Ulysses* was a fortunate thing. So great a writer might otherwise have waited several hundred years to become famous except in the comparatively small group that will go in for a *Ulysses*. But Joyce always considered himself a victim of persecution. I wondered if he was ever that.)

Sullivan wasn't doing so badly as tenor at the Paris Opera House, but he should have been at the Metropolitan or La Scala. Joyce was right about that. He was really one of the great singers of his time, but he apparently fell victim to intrigues in the operatic world and had been rather neglected.

Joyce turned a sympathetic ear to Sullivan's tales of injustice. The banned writer and the banned singer became great friends. After each performance of *Guillaume Tell*, and also of *Les Huguenots*, in which Sullivan sang the role of Raoul, the Joyces and the Sullivans and all of their friends went across the street to the Café de la Paix for supper. The singer, off stage, was very attractive. He was exceedingly touched by Joyce's friendship and by Joyce's determination to gain world recognition for him.

Joyce, who never consented to be interviewed, now consented to talk to reporters—about Sullivan. All the great who knew him but to whom he never bowed were now approached and asked to take up Sullivan. Joyce had made up his mind to get Sullivan into the Metropolitan. But his efforts were fruitless. I saw a certain number of replies to Joyce's appeals: they always said that they would be glad to do anything for Joyce, regretted that they could do nothing for his friend.

Joyce's rather excessive technique at the Paris Opera began to do more harm than good, I fear. For one thing, it got on the nerves of the director. Feelings, perhaps of jealousy, even of patriotism, were stirred up. Sullivan was replaced by the other tenor in the role of William Tell, and Joyce was again obliged to stay away from the opera. Sullivan was alarmed when he found himself practically eliminated from the programs at the Paris Opera. Joyce appealed to all of us. We would call up the box office and book seats for *Guillaume Tell*, maybe a whole box. But we made it clear that it was John Sullivan we wished to hear as Tell. And if we were told it was not to be Sullivan, we canceled the booking. This happened so often that the box office got riled and stopped answering the telephone.

With Joyce, Sullivan's cause became an obsession, and the more he failed the more he persisted in his efforts. Mrs. Joyce got so tired of it that she forbade the mention of Sullivan's name at home.

TWENTY

Away, Away . . .

I was willing to do everything I could for Joyce, but I insisted on going away weekends, and every Saturday there was a tussle with Joyce over my departure for the country. If it hadn't been for Adrienne pulling on my side, I could never have got loose. Joyce, as Saturday approached, always thought up so many extra chores for me that it usually looked as if he were going to win. But Adrienne and my own doggedness to hold on to my Sabbath in the country armed me for resistance.

The weekends were spent in the Eure-et-Loir at the house of Adrienne's parents, Rocfoin. It was on the road to Chartres —you could see the cathedral across the treeless stretch of fields in the wheat-growing country of the Beauce. (Rabelais' explanation of the lack of trees in that country is the most plausible: as the Pantagruel characters rode along, their horses' tails, swishing from side to side, cut down all the trees.)

The Monniers were at some distance from any town, and never seemed to feel the need of a telephone or a car or any other conveniences. On the other hand, they would gladly have traded their thatched roof for tile if the opportunity had offered, but luckily it didn't. I was fond of those lovely mauve-gray straw roofs and was teased by the Monniers for my American preference for anything quaint. If you have plenty of that sort of thing in your life, it hasn't the same charm for you, I suppose.

Sundays were spent in the garden at Rocfoin. A tall elm, one of the rare trees in the region, spread over it like an umbrella. Against the walls grew pears and peaches *en espalier*. There were flowers and poultry, birds and cats, and the two dogs, Mousse and Teddy.

There was no bathroom at Rocfoin. The water supply was from a pump—or you could go across the fields and join the dogs in the tiny river.

At least this weekend place could be reached fairly easily, if you didn't mind walking three miles from the nearest railway station. It was our mountain retreat, Les Déserts, where we spent our summer holiday, that Joyce particularly objected to. As the moment of our departure approached, he would work himself into a state of panic, and up to the last minute presented me with what he called his "grocer's lists," with all the things I was to do for him before I left town. "Many inventions!" I never let anything or anybody interfere with my flight to the Alps, but it was like a game played against a formidable opponent.

It was to the Monniers that I owed the discovery of Les Déserts; Adrienne's mother's people came from this mountain. On its slopes were scattered a lot of little villages, each with its own name but belonging to the community of Les Déserts. The capital, if you can call their center that, possessed a courthouse, schoolhouse, and post office all in one building, a general store, a tobacconist's combined with the cobbler's, and a tavern. To reach the rest of Les Déserts, you had to climb the mountain; a village was on every landing. A last steep pull up and you were on the high Plateau de la Féclaz, to which all the villagers moved with their cattle in the summer, oxcarts carrying a few utensils to their summer quarters. Each of them had a little straw-thatched chalet, or part of one, up there.

It was on this plateau that we spent our vacation, and what

to Joyce were drawbacks—the altitude, about 4,000 feet (he was afraid of high places), the inaccessibility, the lack of postal facilities, of transportation and modern comfort—were the very things we liked about La Féclaz. We didn't even mind the wearying journey one had to take to get there: a night's journey on what the railway ironically called a "*train de plaisir*," a special excursion train to take the Savoyards home to their mountains in the summer to help with the harvest. Nobody but the descendants of people who used to walk all the way to Paris in straw-stuffed wooden sabots to get a job would have let traveling on this train be called a pleasure. But they were very gay and sang the whole time; and I had a close look at my Savoyards.

The first lap of our journey ended early in the morning at Chambéry; the rest of it, more exhausting and very exciting, was ahead. A mountain to climb. It was dark when we reached Les Déserts in a mule wagon.

The tavern where Madame Monnier, Adrienne, and I stayed the first summer I spent at Les Déserts was to be an inn as soon as the second story was built and the beds came; meanwhile, we slept in the hay. Up in the hayloft, the wind, very cold at that altitude, blew through the open space between the roof and the house it sat on; this was to dry the hay. The smell of hay was wonderful, though the blades stuck into your ears like so many knitting needles. The family, our cousins, would have gladly shared their room with us but there were already four people in it.

After the first summer, we were taken in by a couple of the inhabitants, who partitioned off a little bedroom for us in their hayloft. You went up to it by a ladder outside. We were right over the stables, so that we never missed any important events taking place there: a cow having a calf at three in the morning by lantern light, with everybody present; the accident to the pig in the middle of the night, when it was stepped on by a cow and had to be sewed up—a woman, weeping, said he waved one of his paws as if to say, "*adzeu, adzeu*" (patois for *adieu*). At daybreak the stable doors were opened and out poured the cattle like a crowd leaving the theatre. To prevent our being wakened, Adrienne's cousin Fine stuffed paper in the cowbells, but the barking of the dog as he hustled his herd along to the fields—how could she muffle that?

In the hayloft, the corner partitioned off just held two beds; the hay section was our dressing room, and the toilet table was a crate in which Fine kept one or two hens to be fattened up for Sunday dinner. My toothbrush was always falling through the slats onto the poor creatures, and when I poked around among them for it, they squawked.

The chalet, like all the others up there, had been built by the owner, and he had made the furniture also—beds, table, bench, stools, a chair or two. It had a thatched roof. There was a small room on the ground floor, which was the living room, with a kind of closet at the back of it, where they slept. On the north side was a cupboard ventilated by a hole in the wall, where they kept the food; it was almost as good as an icebox. The living room was dimly lighted by a tiny window. To the right of the house door was the stable door; the stable was the larger room of the two. The manure pile was in front of it. The privy was on the side of the chalet next the road, so that you could hold conversations with people passing by.

Fine was a wonderful cook, but there was no meat in those days. We lived well on soup, macaroni, eggs, butter that she herself used to churn, potatoes, and the kind of cheese they make in Savoy called "*tomme.*"

The little chalets scattered over the plateau were exposed to thunderstorms, the terror of the population. If one was struck by a bolt, the thatched roof blazed right up and you had to jump out before you were encircled by a ring of flames as the roof fell in. You had to get the cattle out—the men never left the stable doors as long as a storm was going on. You never even tried to save any of your personal belongings. One stormy summer night, none of us went to bed. Fine burned a candle to the Virgin, and her husband kept close to the stable with a lighted lantern. That night three little chalets were struck at Les Déserts, and nothing was left of them but a pile of stones.

In the evening, neighbors would drop in, the day's work ended. Conversations were in patois and animated; these mountaineers were very vehement. Adrienne knew the patois, and I tried to follow. A haycart had upset coming down the mountain. A cow had fallen down a steep precipice, and it had taken all the men on the plateau to haul her up with ropes from the ledge she had landed on. Some young cow wouldn't have anything to do with Ferdinand's bull. And so on. Sometimes they got on the subject of witches. If asked, they pretended they didn't believe in witchcraft, but in the right mood they would tell of strange doings. There were always certain old women —their names were never mentioned, but everyone knew who they were—who "practiced" and were responsible for things that happened to you. A neighbor had a grudge against you. Your calf died, the butter wouldn't come in the churn, you had a fall. So you knew that your neighbor must have been to see this or that old woman. If you wanted to stop the trouble, a good idea was to boil a lot of rusty nails in a pot, or to take up some of the planks of the floor in the stable and see if a toad might be underneath. The father of one of our friends was pestered with vermin—an hour after he had put on a clean shirt it was covered again with vermin. Seeing an old woman passing the house, he rushed out and seized her by the arm and threatened to beat her unless she took away the curse she had put on him. She was so frightened that she quickly made a certain sign, and he never had another louse.

The dogs, like everybody else, had to work hard for their living at Les Déserts. Their shaggy locks were never washed or combed out. Winter and summer, they spent their days and nights outdoors. They had to keep an eye on their cows, dashing after any that strayed, barking furiously. Their little shepherd masters and mistresses kept them strictly up to the mark. Woe to any dog who didn't jump right up at the call of "*à cu . . . la*"!—at least that's what it sounded like to me.

A sign that a dog was the authentic shepherd breed was when he had one blue eye and the other gray.

We spent our days roaming over the immense pine forests and up and down the hills, enjoying the company of "Chef," who couldn't read or write—he signed his name with a cross.

Telegrams, so important to Joyce, played a small part in the lives of the people of Les Déserts. The postman on his daily rounds brought them with the rest of the mail. No one was taken away from his farm work to bring a telegram all the way up to the Féclaz; it could only be to announce a death, anyway, and the longer it took to reach you, the better. I got one once, and it caused such consternation and distress to the woman we stayed with that I begged the sender, Joyce, to communicate in the future by post only. The postman had handed the woman this wire, looking much concerned over the bad news he was reluctantly conveying to me. She hid it under her apron, and went to ask Adrienne what she was to do with it. While she fetched a bottle of an antishock cordial, always kept on hand for such occasions, Adrienne opened and read the telegram. It was from Joyce and it gave me his next forwarding address.

Joyce's Way of Life

Most of the letters I got from Joyce were, of course, written during my summer holidays or in the course of his own travels. And of course he always demanded replies by "tomorrow," "by express," "by return of post." As a rule, he would be in need of funds, and when I was away, he usually managed to get something through Myrsine, who was left in charge of Shakespeare and Company. As she well knew, whether anything was left in his account or not, we had to look after the author of *Ulysses*.

Joyce's expenses were heavy, naturally, with a family of four, and, besides, he enjoyed spending the way some people enjoy hoarding. A visiting publisher said to me, after dining out with Joyce, "He spends money like a drunken sailor." A funny thing to say, even if it were true, when you had been someone's guest.

Joyce and his family, when they traveled, usually went to places connected with the work he was engaged on at the time. From Belgium, he sent me a series of postcards, reproductions of the mural paintings at the post office. He wrote me that he was making progress in Flemish—he had had his fortieth lesson—and that he had perfected his Dutch. The Joyces crossed the Channel to see Miss Weaver, Mr. Eliot, and Joyce's brother Charles and his old friend from the Zurich days, Frank Budgen. Sometimes the Joyces were accompanied by the Stuart Gilberts, who, however, would never stay with them at the local Palace Hotel. Mr. Gilbert said he couldn't afford to. Neither could the Joyces.

Adrienne and I just managed to make ends meet by living in the simplest style. But Joyce liked to live among the well to do —he wanted to get away as far as he could, no doubt, from the sordidness of the surroundings of his youth. Also, he considered, and rightly, that, with his reputation and achievements, he was entitled to certain material ease, and he spent money freely, loved to throw it away—on others, not himself. Nothing was too good for Nora and the children, and when they traveled, it must be in first-class style.

When you think of Joyce's labors, he was certainly underpaid. And his idea that years of poverty should be followed by many prosperous ones was right; but, then, he should have been a different kind of author.

In Paris, Joyce and his family dined out every evening. His particular restaurant—this was in the early twenties—was the one opposite the Gare Montparnasse, Les Trianons. The proprietor and the entire personnel were devoted to Joyce. They were at the door of his taxi before he alighted and they escorted him to a table reserved for him at the back, where he could be more or less unmolested by people who came to stare at him as he dined, or brought copies of his works to be autographed.

The headwaiter would read to him the items on the bill of fare so that he would be spared the trouble of getting out several pairs of glasses and perhaps a magnifying glass. Joyce pretended to take an interest in fine dishes, but food meant nothing to him, unless it was something to do with his work. He urged his family and the friends who might be dining with him to choose the best food on the menu. He liked to have them eat a hearty meal and persuaded them to try such and such a wine. He himself ate scarcely anything, and was satisfied with the most ordinary white wine just as long as there was plenty of it. As he never drank a drop all day long, he was pretty thirsty by dinnertime. The waiter kept his glass filled. Joyce would have sat there with his family and friends and his white wine till all hours if at a certain moment Nora hadn't decided it was time to go. He ended by obeying her—it was according to an understanding between them, one of the many understandings between this couple who understood each other so well.

Wherever Joyce went, he was received like royalty, such was his personal charm, his consideration for others. When he started on his way downstairs to the men's room, several waiters came hurrying to escort him. His blindness drew people to him a great deal.

Joyce's tips were famous; the waiters, the boy who fetched him a taxi, all those who served him, must have retired with a fortune. I never grudged tips, but, knowing the circumstances, it seemed to me that Joyce overtipped.

All of us who have been guests at Joyce's parties know how hospitable and how amusing he was as host. A most elaborate supper was supplied by one of the best caterers, and a waiter to serve it. Joyce piled food on your plate and filled your glass with his Saint Patrick wine—Clos Saint Patrice, of which once he sent me a crate. Another of his favorites was the Pope's wine —Châteauneuf du Pape; all, of course, on account of the associations. But on the sideboard he kept bottles of his own white wine, and from time to time replenished his glass.

After supper, we would insist that George, or Georgio, as he used to be called, sing for us. Georgio had inherited the family gift, the Voice, to the great satisfaction of his father. He would sing one of his favorites, such as "*Il mio Tesoro*," which was one of my favorites, too.

In the first years, among the few guests invited to these parties were two American couples, great friends of the Joyces: Mr. and Mrs. Richard Wallace and Mr. and Mrs. Myron Nutting. Nutting was an artist, and I wonder what has become of the portrait he drew of Joyce, which I always liked. A friend of George's, Fernandez, whose sister Yva was one of the translators of *Dubliners*, was also one of the guests at the parties in the early period.

In the mid-twenties, when Eugene and Maria Jolas came on the scene, they helped to make Joyce's parties very lively. With her fine voice, Maria Jolas might have had a singer's career, and Joyce was enraptured with her American repertory, particularly with a song he always requested. This was "Farewell Titanic," a rather gruesome but fascinating ditty that, in Maria's dramatic soprano, was most impressive. I noticed that Joyce was quite taken with another of her songs, about someone named "Shy Ann," a character he associated, probably, with his Anna Livia.

Not until the end of the party would Joyce himself be persuaded to wind up the program with some of his Irish songs. He would seat himself at the piano, drooping over the keys, and the old songs, his particular way of singing them in his sweet tenor voice, and the expression on his face—these were things one can never forget.

Joyce never failed to remember people's birthdays, and on

all occasions such as Christmas huge floral offerings turned up, flowers and colors referring to the work he was engaged on at the moment. Adrienne received from him after her publication of "Anna Livia Plurabelle" in the *Navire d'Argent* a magnificently dressed, gigantic cold salmon from Potel and Chabot. Even his gifts to Nora were always related to his books.

TWENTY-ONE

Ulysses Goes to America

Joyce's labors and sacrifices far exceeded his earnings—a sad thing with genius. Joyce's expenses always exceeded his income, and he had moments of panic. And so did Shakespeare and Company. People imagined, perhaps, that I was making a lot of money from *Ulysses*. Well, Joyce must have kept a magnet in his pocket that attracted all the cash Joycewards. I was like Sylvester in the song: "The more I try/ Somehow or other all the coins git by." No one ever said to me, "Sylvester, you keep the change." I understood from the first that, working with or for James Joyce, the pleasure was mine—an infinite pleasure; the profits were for him. All that was available from his work, and I managed to keep it available, was his. But it was all I could do to prevent my bookshop from getting sucked under.

In the summer of 1931, in desperation over the pirating, Joyce asked James Pinker, his agent in London, to get offers for *Ulysses* from publishers in the United States. Offers came, but mostly from firms specializing in erotica. As I remember, the only proposal from a reputable firm was one from Joyce's publisher in the United States, Mr. Huebsch. But he proposed to bring out an expurgated edition of *Ulysses*, and of course Joyce would not consent to that. I regretted very much that

Ulysses couldn't take its place beside *A Portrait of the Artist as a Young Man, Dubliners,* and *Exiles* on Mr. Huebsch's list.

Most of the other offers from would-be publishers of *Ulysses* rounded up by Pinker seemed uninteresting to both Joyce and me, and neither of us liked the tone of the letters that accompanied them.

These offers were addressed to Shakespeare and Company as Joyce's *representative* in Paris, not as his publisher. And apparently this was according to Joyce's instructions to Pinker. It was exactly as if they were proposing to publish a manuscript, not to take over a book that had been published by somebody else for almost ten years. This didn't seem to me the correct way to do things, and I waited for Joyce to speak up, but he never did. I was as anxious as he was to see *Ulysses,* the greatest of contemporary books, brought out in the English-speaking countries, freed of the disgraceful label of "banned book," and made available to the general public. It didn't occur to me that I might receive something when a suitable arrangement was made for the publication of *Ulysses* in my country—until I realized that it hadn't occurred to anyone else. Then I began to be exasperated at being ignored. I told Joyce so; I also pointed out that it would look better if I did not appear simply to be dumping *Ulysses,* and asked him if he didn't think I should demand something. He neither encouraged nor discouraged me—so in my reply to the next offer that came in I said that I would expect to receive something for relinquishing my rights. The person from whom that particular offer had come wrote back to ask what I would demand. Twenty-five thousand dollars, said I. This of course made him and everybody who saw it later, when the Pinker correspondence was made public, burst out laughing. (I explained to Joyce that my figure was only a proof of my esteem for the book.) When I asked this merchant what he would consider a fair sum, he wouldn't name it, nor did anyone else have the idea for a moment that my claim was serious.

There was one important exception. Mr. Huebsch kindly

MEMORANDUM OF AGREEMENT made this nineth day
of December, 1930 BETWEEN James Joyce, Esquire,
c/o Shakespeare & Co., 12 Rue de l'Odéon, Paris
(Hereinafter called the Author) of the one part
and Miss Sylvia Beach, Shakespeare and Company,
12 Rue de l'Odeon, Paris (Hereinafter called the
Publisher) of the other part, whereby it is
agreed by and between the parties as follows:

THE AUTHOR HEREBY AGREES:

    I.   To assign to the Publisher the
exclusive right of printing and selling throughout
the world, the work entitled ULYSSES.

THE PUBLISHER HEREBY AGREES:

    I.   To print and publish at her own risk
and expense the said Work

    2.   To pay the Author on all copies sold
a royalty on the published price of twenty-five
per cent.

    3.   To abandon the right to said Work if,
after due consideration such a step should be
deemed advisable by the Author and the Publisher
in the interests of the AUTHOR, in which case,
the right to publish said Work shall be purchased
from the Publisher at the price set by herself,
to be paid by the publishers acquiring the right
to publish said Work.

Facsimile of the contract for ULYSSES

offered to pay me a royalty. But there was no question of my accepting it, because it would have come out of Joyce's royalty. I wouldn't have considered that for a moment. Neither, for that matter, would Joyce, and rightly, I think.

Contracts didn't seem important to either Joyce or myself. At the time I published *Ulysses*, I did mention the subject, but Joyce wouldn't hear of a contract and I didn't care, so I never brought up the question again. But in 1927, when I brought out *Pomes Penyeach*, Joyce himself asked me to have a contract drawn up; and in 1930 he suddenly wanted a contract for *Ulysses*, too. The wording of these contracts was as Joyce wanted it. He read and approved them, and he signed them. The paper of the contract for *Ulysses* was stamped, official stationery. To be sure, it wasn't witnessed by an "*avoué*," but nobody seemed to think that necessary.

I think Joyce's purpose in having this contract between us all of a sudden must have been to prove, in a matter in which he was engaged at the time, that *Ulysses* was not his property but mine. In a letter to the lawyer who was prosecuting the pirate of *Ulysses*, Joyce stated plainly that *Ulysses* was not his property but belonged to Sylvia Beach. I had never seen this letter of Joyce's till lately, when it was shown to me.

Offers for a bargain sale of *Ulysses* stopped coming in, and I didn't see Joyce for a time. But nearly every day I saw an old friend of his, who dropped in from the Square Robiac to give me his views on the subject of a new publisher for *Ulysses*. He urged me to relinquish what I imagined were my claims. "But what about our contract?" I asked one day. "Is that imaginary?" "That's no contract," said the friend—he was a poet and one I had admired since my teens. "It doesn't exist, your contract." And, when I contradicted this statement, he made a remark that immediately floored me. "You're standing in the way of Joyce's interests." That was what he said.

As soon as he had left the bookshop, I telephoned to Joyce. I told him that he was now free to dispose of *Ulysses* in any way that suited him and that I would make no further claims on it.

I think that Joyce may already have been discussing an arrangement with Random House through someone in his family, though nothing was said to me about it. And with so much at stake, perhaps Joyce's way of going about the American publication of *Ulysses* was the best way.

Joyce himself informed me, when *Ulysses* came out—the fine Random House edition, with Judge John M. Woolsey's verdict of acquittal for this great work, was sent to me—that he had already received $45,000 from the publishers. I know how desperately he needed the money. The expenses of his daughter's illness were increasing, and there was his failing eyesight. I felt an immense joy over his good fortune, which was to put an end to his financial troubles. As for my personal feelings, well, one is not at all proud of them, and they should be promptly dumped when they no longer serve a purpose.

Neither of our contracts was of the slightest use to me. There was some mention in them of an arrangement with Shakespeare and Company if these works were taken over by other publishers, but the transfer of both *Ulysses* and *Pomes Penyeach* took place quite independently of their original publisher. However, in the case of *Ulysses*, I gave Joyce leave to do whatever he wished. And, after all, the books were Joyce's. A baby belongs to its mother, not to the midwife, doesn't it?

Joyce tried to persuade me to bring out a cheap Continental edition of *Ulysses*, but I couldn't get interested in this idea. I was too hard up, and it would also have meant continuing my services to him—which was impossible because my bookshop needed me very much and besides I was tired. About that time I had a visit from one of the members of the Odyssey Press, and he accepted with alacrity my suggestion that he ask Joyce's consent to bring out a Continental edition. The Odyssey Press was, I think, a branch of the Tauchnitz editions, in which *A Portrait of the Artist as a Young Man* had already appeared. Joyce accepted the offer of the Odyssey Press. I informed them that my contract was only an affair between Joyce and themselves, but these decent people insisted on giving me a royalty, and, since it didn't affect Joyce's royalty, I accepted. The Odyssey Press edition was very attractive, and this time Stuart Gilbert corrected the errors.

Meanwhile, taxifuls of Joyce business were transferred from Shakespeare and Company to Paul Léon, the very good friend of Joyce who looked after the Joyce business henceforth.

The Thirties

By the thirties, the Left Bank had changed. The so-called "lost generation"—I can't think of a generation less deserving of this name—had grown up and become famous. Many of my friends had gone home. I missed them, and I missed the fun of discovery and the little reviews and the little publishing houses. It had been pleasanter emerging from a war than going toward another one, and of course there was the depression. But we still had a few of our best friends around the Quarter, at least for a time. Hemingway had an apartment near Saint Sulpice; the MacLeishes planned to settle down near the Luxembourg Gardens. We had had to part with Pound, who preferred Rapallo, but still we had Joyce, Eugene and Maria Jolas and *transition*, and Gertrude Stein and Alice B. Toklas in the rue Christine. And in the rue Notre Dame des Champs, where Hemingway, in his rooms above a sawmill, had produced some of his first stories and Ezra Pound used to be seen in his velvet beret coming in and out of his studio, Katherine Anne Porter occuped a *pavillon*.

Katherine Anne had a handsome tomcat named Skipper. His mistress was such a good cook that Skipper began to lose his figure. She invented a sort of Swedish system, with pulleys attached to a tree, that forced Skipper to do exercises in the garden. But Skipper was not the slim type.

One day Skipper had a narrow escape. He was sitting at the street gate observing passers-by—and his mistress came out just in time to see a woman putting him into a large basket. "But wait," she cried, "that's my cat!" In another minute it would have been too late. Many plump cats disappear in Paris; they make such nice rabbit stews.

My friend Carlotta Welles (Mrs. James Briggs) invited Katherine Anne Porter to speak at the American Women's Club in Paris. I don't like "talks" as a rule, but this one, like everything Katherine Anne Porter says or writes, was fascinating. She gave me the typescript of her notes to keep.

Allen Tate was one of my friends of the late twenties, when he first came to Paris on a fellowship. Now, with Caroline Tate, he was again in Paris, and I used to see him often with Katherine Anne Porter. I think these two represent something very much apart and very important in our writing today. In the summing up of the poetry of his generation, I wonder if Allen Tate won't be given a high place. I have found several of the others quite interesting and original, and their inventions sometimes amazing, but with Allen Tate's poetry I feel as pleased as, say, when I read some good English poet.

During the twenties, and louder in the thirties, one heard rumblings from the Villa Seurat, the Henry Miller center of the Left Bank. Henry Miller and that lovely Japanese-looking friend of his, Miss Anaïs Nin, came to see if I would publish an interesting novel he had been working on, *Tropic of Cancer*. I suggested that they show the manuscript to Jack Kahane, who accepted with pleasure this work by a new writer, something that combined literary and sex value. Kahane was fond of a certain forthright sexiness. He brought out *Tropic of Cancer* and *Tropic of Capricorn*, and other works by Miller. I liked

a volume of essays by Miller, *The Hamlet*, which was published
at the Villa Seurat. Then there was a booklet entitled *Money
and How It Gets That Way*, a rather Poundian title. The last
word I had from that center was "an open letter to all and
sundry" entitled *What Are You Going to Do About Alf?*
Almost immediately you were informed that it had been done.

Thomas Wolfe came over to Paris and to the bookshop just
after *Of Time and the River* was published. He said Max
Perkins had handed him a check and put him on a boat bound
for Europe. He talked about the influence of Joyce on his
work; he was trying to get out from under it, he said. Wolfe
was indubitably a young man of genius, and perhaps very un-
satisfactory as a social being. Mrs. Adelaide Massey, to whom
he had a letter, mothered him while he was in Paris, and he
needed it.

My dear Mrs. Massey, a friend of the poor and of mine, was
a native of Middleburg, Virginia. She divided her time between
her studies at the British Institute, her benevolent work with
Sister Mary Reeves, of whom she was the right hand, and her
benevolent work at Shakespeare and Company. (She is still in
the relief work started by Ann Morgan, and has been awarded
the Legion of Honor.) She was interested in writing—other
people's. She herself had a definite gift, and everybody but Mrs.
Massey was convinced that she could and should write.

At a time when I had no one to help me in the bookshop,
Mrs. Massey came every day to the rescue. And when I had
a young assistant who was always coming down with children's
diseases, Mrs. Massey luckily was on hand to fill the breach. I
was absent once for a few days. I came back to find that Shakespeare and Company's assistant had measles and had been taken
to the hospital in an ambulance; Mrs. Massey was busy fumigat-
ing the premises.

I was never able to afford to pay my assistants enough to
make it worth their while, but I was fortunate enough to have

friends who could put up with me and the other drawbacks of life in my bookshop.

From the beginning and right through the thirties and on into the forties, someone was always coming along to be the assistant at Shakespeare and Company. The first two helpers were volunteers, Lucie Schwoff and Susanne Malherbe. Then there was Myrsine Moschos, who worked with me for nine years. The first and only really professional assistant I ever had was Miss Jane van Meter, now Mrs. Charlton Hinman—her husband is a Shakespearean expert. I put an ad in the Paris *Herald Tribune*, and Miss van Meter answered it. I couldn't wish anybody better luck than to have her as an assistant.

Late in the thirties, in spite of threats of war, my lovely godchild from Chicago, Sylvia Peter, came over to study in Paris and to help me in the bookshop. She was succeeded by the very competent Eleanor Oldenburger. Then it was the turn of a charming young girl, Priscilla Curtiss, with whom I parted reluctantly. She would have stayed but the war was at hand.

After the war began and up to the Occupation, a brilliant young French woman, Madame Paulette Lévy, whose husband was at the front came regularly to help me. A Canadian student, Ruth Camp, who could not be persuaded to leave in spite of my efforts to push her homeward, was still helping me when the Germans swarmed into France.

Friends of Shakespeare and Company

The bookshop was now famous. It was always crowded with new and old customers, and was written up more and more in the newspapers and magazines. It was even pointed out to American Express tourists as they passed—in buses that stopped in front of No. 12 for a couple of seconds. Nevertheless, Shakespeare and Company was beginning to be seriously hit by the depression. Our business, which, with the departure of my compatriots, had already suffered, rapidly declined. My

French friends remained, and they might have filled the gap left by my homeward-going customers but they, too, had been affected by the depression.

By the middle of the thirties, the situation was quite alarming, and one day in 1936 when André Gide dropped in to ask how we were getting along, I told him that I was thinking of putting up the shutters. Gide was aghast over this news. "We can't give up Shakespeare and Company!" he exclaimed, and dashed across the street to ask Adrienne Monnier if what I had told him was true. Alas! she could only confirm it.

Immediately, Gide got a group of writers together to plan my rescue. The first idea they had was to petition the French government to subsidize Shakespeare and Company. The petition was signed by the writers and also by eminent professors at the Sorbonne, but funds were lacking, especially for the support of a foreign enterprise such as mine. A committee was then formed composed of Georges Duhamel, Luc Durtain, André Gide, Louis Gillet, Jacques de Lacretelle, André Maurois, Paul Morand, Jean Paulhan, Jules Romains, Jean Schlumberger, and Paul Valéry. It was my good friend Schlumberger who wrote the appeal, in a bulletin the committee had printed, to save my bookshop. It was proposed that two hundred friends subscribe two hundred francs a year for two years. By that time, surely, Shakespeare and Company would be on its feet again. The writers on the committee undertook to read in turn at the bookship an unpublished work. These readings were to take place about once a month. Subscribers, as members of The Friends of Shakespeare and Company, would be entitled to attend the readings. Subscribers were limited to two hundred because that was the largest number of people who could be stuffed into the little shop. Many more than two hundred would have liked to be members, and some of my friends gave special contributions: Mrs. James Briggs, Bryher, Miss Marian Willard, Miss Ann Morgan, Mrs. W. F. Peter, Mrs. Helena Rubinstein, Mr. Archibald MacLeish, and Mr. James Hill.

The first reading was by André Gide, who chose his play *Geneviève*. He was followed by Jean Schlumberger, reading from an unpublished novel, *Saint Saturnin*. Next came Jean Paulhan, director of the *Nouvelle Revue Française* and great philologist. He read the first part of a new work, *Les Fleurs de Tarbes*, an interesting but almost totally incomprehensible work. We all had to acknowledge that it was beyond us— except my young errand girl, who said that she had understood every word! André Maurois read a delightful unpublished story, and Paul Valéry some of his most beautiful verses, including *"Le Serpent"* at Joyce's special request. I was very much touched when T. S. Eliot came over from London to read at Shakespeare and Company. Ernest Hemingway for once made an exception to his rule against reading in public and consented to appear if Stephen Spender could be persuaded to join him. So we had a double reading, and a great sensation it made!

By this time we were so glorious with all these famous writers and all the press articles that we began to do very well in business.

Since my friends were doing so much for me, I thought I should sacrifice something myself. I decided to sell some of my most precious treasures. I began by approaching a well-known firm in London on the subject of a sale. They were extremely interested in the list I sent them, and the arrangements were being made when at my request they inquired whether there might be a risk of seizure of the Joyce, particularly the *Ulysses*, items. They were informed that this might well happen, and reluctantly we agreed to abandon the sale.

It was after this episode that I issued a little catalogue of my own. Perhaps this catalogue failed to reach the Joyce collectors—or perhaps few were collecting Joyce in the thirties. At any rate, most of the letters I got asked whether I had anything of Hemingway's. I parted reluctantly with my cherished "firsts" of Hemingway, with their valued inscriptions.

On a trip to the United States at about this time, I visited my friend Miss Marian Willard, now Mrs. Dan Johnson of the Willard Gallery, in New York. I relinquished to her my set of the corrected proofs of *Ulysses*. And Professor Theodore Spencer acquired for Harvard the first manuscript of *A Portrait of the Artist* (*Stephen Hero*). The manuscripts of *Chamber Music*, *Dubliners*, and *Pomes Penyeach* were the next to go. This was not, however, until I had lost all hope of finding some way of keeping all of the Joyce items together. Sadly, I yielded to necessity, but it was painful.

"Expo 1937"

I never went in much for fairs, but the Paris "Expo 1937" was different. The Minister of Education at the moment was an admirer of Paul Valéry, and the poet was asked to organize an exhibition of French writing. He was given a whole pavilion in which to display the documents illustrating the modern movement from its beginnings to the latest developments. This section of the fair was very popular, crowded from morning till night. Adrienne's publications were, of course, among the exhibitions, but since this was an all-French affair, mine were excluded. Nevertheless, I had a stand, in the press section, for the English review *Life and Letters Today*, for which Shakespeare and Company was the Paris distributor. It was at Bryher's request that I became an exhibitor at the "Expo." The current number of *Life and Letters* was prominently placed, with a lot of bright-colored specimen covers and publicity material, between the venerable *Revue de Deux Mondes* and the children's favorite magazine, *Mickey Mouse*.

Life and Letters Today was active in spreading French letters in England. It had published translations of Gide, Valéry, Michaux, and others in previous numbers; its current issue, in honor of the exposition, was an all-French number.

TWENTY-TWO

War and the Occupation

Up in Savoy at the end of the summer of 1939, posters summoned all the young men to join their regiments, and there was great mourning in all of the families. I took the last bus down the mountain before the young driver was mobilized and the bus requisitioned. The station at Chambéry was crowded with soldiers carrying their equipment. I managed to get on a train to Paris. In the same compartment was a young Englishwoman with her baby and her nurse. They were hurrying home to England. The husband had said good-by on the platform. He would follow his family soon, but he didn't believe we'd have war.

Shakespeare and Company remained open. The war went on. Then suddenly the Germans swept over France. As they came nearer and nearer to Paris, the population fled or tried to flee. Day and night, people streamed through the rue de l'Odéon. People camped, and slept, in front of the railway stations in the hope of getting on a train. Some left in their cars—which had to be abandoned along the roadsides for lack of gas. Most of them fled on foot, carrying babies and baggage, or pushing baby carriages or wheelbarrows. Some had bicycles. Meanwhile, a constant stream of refugees from the north and northeast, including Belgium—people uprooted from their farms and towns—flowed through the city toward the west.

Adrienne and I did not join the exodus. Why flee? My Canadian student assistant, Ruth Camp, did try to get away. She was machine-gunned in the ditches, and was later interned in spite of her efforts.

A lovely June day in 1940. Sunny with blue skies. Only about 25,000 people were left in Paris. Adrienne and I went over to the Boulevard Sébastopol and, through our tears, watched the refugees moving through the city. They came in at the East Gate, crossed Paris by way of the Boulevard Saint Michel and the Luxembourg Gardens, then went out through the Orléans and Italie gates: cattle-drawn carts piled with household goods; on top of them children, old people and sick people, pregnant women and women with babies, poultry in coops, and dogs and cats. Sometimes they stopped at the Luxembourg Gardens to let the cows graze there.

From the windows in the hospital where I had lunch with my old friend Dr. Bertrand-Fontaine, we watched the last of the refugees pouring in. Close on their heels came the Germans. An endless procession of motorized forces: tanks and armored cars and helmeted men seated with arms folded. The men and the machines were all a cold gray, and they moved to a steady deafening roar.

There were a few Nazi sympathizers in Paris, called "*Collabos*," but they were the exception. Everybody we knew was for resistance. Dr. Bertrand-Fontaine was an active member of the Resistance. Her son Rémi died at twenty in one of the worst prison camps, Mauthausen in Austria.

Parisians who survived the exodus came back, and my French friends were delighted to find Shakespeare and Company still open. They fairly stuffed themselves on our books, and I was busier than ever. I had a volunteer helper, a young Jewish friend, Françoise Bernheim. A student of Sanscrit, but now excluded from the Sorbonne by the Nazi laws, she was encouraged by her professor to copy the notes taken by her non-Jewish friends, and, with his help and theirs, she was persevering in her studies.

I had resisted all the efforts of my Embassy to persuade me to return to the United States. (The route was through Lisbon, and the alluring rates for transportation included the item: "a parrot, six dollars.") Instead, I had settled down to share life in Nazi-occupied Paris with my friends. Also, as I went about with Françoise, I shared with her some of the special restrictions on Jews—though not the large yellow Star of David that she wore on her coat or dress. We went about on bicycles, the only form of transportation. We could not enter public places such as theatres, movies, cafés, concert halls, or sit down on park benches or even on those in the streets. Once, we tried taking our lunch to a shady square. Sitting on the ground *beside* a bench, we hurriedly ate our hard-boiled eggs and swallowed the tea in our thermos bottles, looking around furtively as we did so. It was not an experience that we cared to repeat.

Shakespeare and Company Vanishes

When the United States came into the war, my nationality, added to my Jewish affiliations, finished Shakespeare and Company in Nazi eyes. We Americans had to declare ourselves at the Kommandatur and register once a week at the Commissary in the section of Paris where we lived. (Jews had to sign every day.) There were so few Americans that our names were in a sort of scrapbook that was always getting mislaid. I used to find it for the Commissaire. Opposite my name and antecedents was the notation: "has no horse." I could never find out why.

My German customers were always rare, but of course after I was classified as "the enemy," they stopped coming altogether —until a last outstanding visit ended the series. A high-ranking

German officer, who had got out of a huge gray military car, stopped to look at a copy of *Finnegans Wake* that was in the window. Then he came in and, speaking perfect English, said he would buy it. "It's not for sale." "Why not?" My last copy, I explained. I was keeping it. For whom? For myself. He was angry. He was so interested in Joyce's work, he said. Still I was firm. Out he strode, and I removed *Finnegans Wake* from the window and put it safely away.

A fortnight later, the same officer strode into the bookshop. Where was *Finnegans Wake*? I had put it away. Fairly trembling with rage, he said, "We're coming to confiscate all your goods today." "All right." He drove off.

I consulted my concierge. She opened an unoccupied apartment on the third floor. (My own apartment was on the second floor.) My friends and I carried all the books and all the photographs upstairs, mostly in clothesbaskets; and all the furniture. We even removed the electric-light fixtures. I had a carpenter take down the shelves. Within two hours, not a single thing was to be seen in the shop, and a house painter had painted out the name, Shakespeare and Company, on the front of 12 rue de l'Odéon. The date was 1941. Did the Germans come to confiscate Shakespeare and Company's goods? If so, they never found the shop.

Eventually, they did come to fetch the proprietor of Shakespeare and Company.

After six months in an internment camp, I was back in Paris, but with a paper stating that I could be taken again by the German military authorities at any time they saw fit. My friends agreed that, instead of waiting to be sent back, I should "disappear." Miss Sarah Watson undertook to hide me in her Foyer des Etudiantes (Students' Hostel) at 93 Boulevard Saint Michel. I lived happily in the little kitchen at the top of the house with Miss Watson and her assistant, Madame Marcelle Fournier. With the card I was given as a member of the Foyer, I felt as though I was back in my student days. The Germans had made several attempts to take over the Foyer, but, though

Miss Watson herself was interned for a time, Madame Fournier performed the miracle of keeping the place open and full of students going on with their studies. It was American, with an American head, but, since it was attached to the University of Paris, the Recteur obtained the release of Miss Watson from the internment camp and she continued at her post.

I visited the rue de l'Odéon daily, secretly, heard the latest news of Adrienne's bookshop, saw the latest volume of the clandestine Editions de Minuit. The Midnight Editions, which had a wide underground circulation, were published by my friend Yvonne Desvignes at terrible risk. All of the prominent writers in the Resistance appeared in it. Eluard used to deliver the little volumes.

TWENTY-THREE

The Liberation

The Liberation of Paris was nearly complete—it depended on the quarter you inhabited whether or not you were free of the Germans. Ours, in the neighborhood of the Luxembourg Place and Gardens, where the SS troops were intrenched, was one of the last to get rid of the Occupation.

As soon as the 14th Arrondissement was freed, we had a jubilating visit from Adrienne's brother-in-law, Bécat. He came on his bicycle, which was ornamented with a little French flag. It happened to be the worst day in our quarter. He arrived just in time to see, from my windows, the old Hôtel Corneille, nearby in the rue Corneille, go up in flames. The Germans had used it as offices, and, when they left, they destroyed it, with all their papers. I was particularly fond of the Hôtel Corneille because Joyce had stayed there as a student—his notebook of the period is now in the Lockwood Library in Buffalo—and, before Joyce, Yeats and Synge.

Bécat's congratulations came too soon. He had to go back by way of the cellars, carrying his bicycle. The cellars, according to civil-defense orders, were made to open into each other.

In the mornings, toward 11 o'clock, the Nazis sallied forth from the Luxembourg with their tanks and went down the

Boulevard Saint Michel, shooting here and there. Rather dis-
agreeable for those of us who were lined up at the bakery at
the bread hour. Another thing I didn't like was the shooting
up and down our own street. The children engaged in our
defense piled up furniture, stoves, garbage cans, and so on at
the foot of the rue de l'Odéon, and behind these barricades
youths with F.F.I. armbands and a strange assortment of old-
fashioned weapons aimed at the Germans stationed on the
steps of the theatre at the top of the street. These soldiers
were rather dangerous, but the boys in the Resistance were
fearless and they played an important part in the Liberation of
Paris.

I finally left the Students' Hostel and went back to the rue
de l'Odéon to stay. Going to and fro was getting too unpleasant. Adrienne and I gave up going out at all after a frightening experience. We heard that "they" were leaving us, and we
joined a jolly crowd of Parisians walking down the Boulevard
Saint Michel singing and waving w.c. brushes. We were feeling very joyful and liberated. But "they" happened to be leaving at the same moment, pouring down the street with the
remnants of their motorized forces. "They" didn't like the
celebration, lost their tempers, and began machine-gunning the
crowds on the sidewalks. Like everybody else, Adrienne and
I lay flat on our bellies and edged over to the nearest doorway.
When the shooting stopped and we got up, we saw blood on
the pavements and Red Cross stretchers picking up the casu-
alties.

Hemingway Liberates the Rue de l'Odéon

There was still a lot of shooting going on in the rue de
l'Odéon, and we were getting tired of it, when one day a
string of jeeps came up the street and stopped in front of my
house. I heard a deep voice calling: "Sylvia!" And everybody
in the street took up the cry of "Sylvia!"

"It's Hemingway! It's Hemingway!" cried Adrienne. I flew downstairs; we met with a crash; he picked me up and swung me around and kissed me while people on the street and in the windows cheered.

We went up to Adrienne's apartment and sat Hemingway down. He was in battle dress, grimy and bloody. A machine gun clanked on the floor. He asked Adrienne for a piece of soap, and she gave him her last cake.

He wanted to know if there was anything he could do for us. We asked him if he could do something about the Nazi snipers on the roof tops in our street, particularly on Adrienne's roof top. He got his company out of the jeeps and took them up to the roof. We heard firing for the last time in the rue de l'Odéon. Hemingway and his men came down again and rode off in their jeeps—"to liberate," according to Hemingway, "the cellar at the Ritz."

over-compensating?

INDEX